Green
HOMES

Green
HOMES

Sergi Costa Duran

Introduction by:

Lance Hosey

COLLINS DESIGN

An Imprint of HarperCollins Publishers

HarperCollins books may be purchased for educational, business, or sales promotional use.
For information, please write: Special Markets Department, HarperCollins*Publishers,*
10 East 53rd Street, New York, NY 10022.

First published in 2007 by:
Collins Design
An Imprint of HarperCollins*Publishers*
10 East 53rd Street
New York, NY 10022
Tel.: (212) 207-7000
Fax: (212) 207-7654
collinsdesign@harpercollins.com
www.harpercollins.com

Distributed throughout the world by:
HarperCollins*Publishers*
10 East 53rd Street
New York, NY 10022
Fax: (212) 207-7654

Packaged by:
LOFT Publications
Via Laietana, 32, 4.° Of. 92
08003 Barcelona, Spain
Tel.: +34 932 688 088
Fax: +34 932 687 073
loft@loftpublications.com
www.loftpublications.com

Editor and texts:
Sergi Costa Duran

Editorial assistant:
Aitana Lleonart

Editorial coordination:
Catherine Collin

Translation:
Cillero & De Motta

Art director:
Mireia Casanovas Soley

Cover:
Claudia Martínez Alonso

Layout:
Yolanda G. Román

Library of Congress Control Number: 2007933298

ISBN: 978-0-06-134826-6

Printed in Spain
Fourth Printing, 2010

First, there grew up in the courtyard an olive tree. Round that olive tree I built a chamber, and I roofed it well and set doors to it. Then I sheared off all the light wood on the growing olive tree, and I rough-hewed the trunk with the adze, and I made the tree into a bed post. Beginning with this bed post I wrought a bedstead, and when I finished it, I inlaid it with silver and ivory. Such was the bed I built for myself, and such a bed could not be moved to this place or that.

—Odyssey, Homer

Today, at sunrise, we saw a white flame among the trees, high on a sheer peak before us. We thought that it was a fire and we stopped. The flame was unmoving, yet blinding as liquid metal. So we climbed toward it through the rocks. And there, before us, on a broad summit, with the mountains rising behind it, stood a house such as we had never seen, and the white fire came from the sun on the glass of its windows....The house had two stories and a strange roof flat as a floor. There was more window than wall upon its walls, and the windows went on straight around the corners, though how this kept the house standing we could not guess.

—Anthem, Ayn Rand

THE ECOLOGY OF HOME

Lance Hosey

These two passages, written nearly three thousand years apart, represent dramatically different concepts of home.

In the first, from Homer's Odyssey (c. 800 BC), the hero describes how he built his bed chamber. Returning after two decades away, Odysseus is not recognized. As if to reintroduce himself to his own household, he recounts how he founded the estate. Having carefully crafted its centerpiece, the bedstead, around a living olive tree, he created a house that "could not be moved to this place or that." For him, home is rooted in place.

Contrast this with the second narrative, from the novel Anthem (1937). Ayn Rand's most reactionary critique of socialism, the story is a dystopian parable in which the community so outweighs the individual that the concept of self has disappeared altogether. The single-family house has vanished along with the single family. The narrator, who refers to himself as we, because the word I has been forgotten, escapes the fortress commune and retreats to a mountainous outland, where he discovers "a house such as we [he] had never seen." Looking glasses, narrow doorways, a personal library, and a bedroom too small for more than two all signal a lifestyle for the few, not the many. In this "place of wonders," the narrator rediscovers individuality and private life.

While both stories ask fundamental questions about identity and home, their answers are very different.

Homer portrays the house as entangled in its environment, inextricable from the living tree. Rand conceives the house as a vessel for the self—a solipsistic refuge. Over the entry the protagonist of Anthem carves "the sacred word": ego. Homer's house extrudes itself from the earth. Rand's floats like a flame. The ancient home was bound to its natural setting; by nature it was externalized, a reflection of its surroundings. The modern was internalized, a personal sanctuary.

This distinction is not between old and new but between house and home. A house is just shelter—four walls and a roof— but home, of course, is where the heart is. In this sense, the concept of a green home is essentially redundant. While green building strategies

Farnsworth House © Jon Miller, Hedrich Blessing
Photographers courtesy of Landmarks Illinois

Johnson Glass House
© Michael Moran

often focus on technical issues such as energy efficiency and material content, sustainability really is a form of homecoming. The Greek root of ecology, oikos, means "home," an understanding of place familiar to indigenous peoples. Native American activist Winona LaDuke describes the task of sustainability using the Anishinaabeg word keewaydahn—"going home." Ecology is rooted in home, and home is rooted in place, so green home has a circular definition.

The relationship between a house and its ecosystem mirrors the relationship between home and planet. Whereas the boundaries of a house may lie at its property line, home includes the entire earth. As Thoreau mused, "What's the use of a house if you haven't got a tolerable planet to put it on?" A house does not become a home through dramatic design but through a profound empathy between people and place.

Yet, the rooted nature of home is lost on the modernist conception of both house and culture. In philosophy and practice, the Industrial Revolution attempted to subdue nature, and Freud called the "exploitation of the earth" one of the hallmarks of culture. Nature had value only through human permission. Rand has her character claim that "the sight of my eyes grants beauty to the earth," and he controls everything he sees: "my sky, my forest, this earth of mine." This possessive attitude toward the earth is well represented by the "house such as we had never seen"—a Miesian glass box, which would have seemed so futuristic in 1937.(How quaint to call

a flat roof strange.) The modernist glass house transformed the picture window —nature as decoration—into an entire building. "There was more window than wall upon its walls," as Rand describes it. From safe inside, the rest of life was a thing to behold, like a souvenir. Look, don't touch.

Ironic that for her chapel of individuality Rand would choose the machine aesthetic, an architectural vocabulary based on mechanical reproduction. Her house-of-the-self sounds much like Philip Johnson's house for himself, built in Connecticut a decade later (1949). But Johnson's personal expression was dependent on someone else's personality, since he was admittedly Mies van der Rohe's ventriloquist's dummy. Consequently, his house was more homage than home, and it has always felt more like a museum than a residence. The architect is said to have been "distracted" by its "proximity to nature," and this sort of distraction seems to have been endemic to the modernist house. Mies's own version of his vision, the glass-walled Farnsworth House (1951), was abandoned by Edith Farnsworth within six months because she felt exposed, alienated, or alone. This house literally became a museum.

Frank Lloyd Wright replaced Mies as Rand's inspiration in her most popular novel, The Fountainhead (1943), which itself carved out ego as the sacred word of the architect. In seven years, Rand seems to have realized that the self in question is not the occupant but the architect. Since then, the designer house has become an excuse to live out the architect's dreams, not accommodate those of the client or the commu-

nity. As anyone who has ever lived in a Wright house will tell you, this kind of structure is more the domain of the designer than the owner.

Of course, most American houses are driven not by egoism but by economics, since the majority sit in commercial real estate developments. The premodern house was wedded to place, embodying its larger setting through local materials, local techniques, local climate, and local culture. Think of the Thai thatch hut, the Inuit igloo, the Icelandic turf farm, the Nantucket saltbox, the Virginia dogtrot, the Anasazi cliff dwelling. In the hands of contemporary production builders, regional flavor has become a brand to be marketed anywhere, and the image of place has become independent of the actual place. An English manor made sense in Oxford but not in Albuquerque, and a Tudor in Tallahassee symbolizes the comforts of home without providing them. Today, true International Style is not based on the machine aesthetic—it's the McMansion. When home becomes a commodity, the entire planet becomes a suburb of Dallas.

How do we address the dilemma of home in an age of environmental and cultural degradation? How can home transcend the glamorization of the architect and the globalization of place? The book in your hands asks these questions. In various ways—with varying degrees of success—every project examines identity in relation to social and natural community. If this work is any indication, the modern green home is a tug-of-war between place and personality.

The subject of that last sentence was carefully chosen because the focus of this book is not the green home but the modern(ist) green home. Every project dates from the last five years, and virtually all of them adopt the formal traits of modernism even while challenging its technical and philosophical premises. These architects explore the relationships between aesthetics and ethics by combining Mies's "less is more" dictum with environmentalist Paul Hawken's description of sustainability as "doing more with less."

Though diverse in size and situation, together the projects illustrate four kinds of inquiry:

- Technique. How is it made?
- Systems. How does it perform?
- Aesthetics. What does it look like?
- Context. How does it relate to its natural and cultural environment?

Context varies considerably, as twelve projects are spread across North America, nine through Europe, and two in Australia. Most are detached single-family houses, two are multi-housing units, and a few defy categorization. (Baumraum's Between Alder and Oak tree house marries Homer's tree-bound home to Rand's floating glass box).

Much of the work is exceptional. Jennifer Siegal's Seatrain House is one of the most compelling residential designs in recent memory. Salvaging materials has become popular, but the designs often appear stitched together like a junkyard Frankenstein. The Seatrain transcends its bits and pieces and trans-

forms an industrial wasteland into a gorgeous oasis, a home on the scrap heap. Kieran Timberlake's Loblolly House combines mechanical fabrication with a uniquely sensitive interpretation of its wooded setting. The blending of the striated cladding with the surrounding pine forest seems to cause figure and ground to oscillate in a way that is positively surreal.

Some of these projects apply environmental strategies to old forms. The Les-Gwen McDonald House is a Canadian modern version of McKim, Mead, and White's Low House. The lacing of brick and photovoltaic panels in the Solaire, by Pelli Clark Pelli, echoes both the Manhattan tradition of layered highrise facades as well as Cesar Pelli's own long-term interest in expressing the thinness of modern construction. EHDD's F10 house updates the Chicago town house, Arkin Tilt's Eastern Sierra House reinterprets the Western cabin, House W reimagines a Bavarian farm, R4 House brings the Japanese metabolism to Spain, and Domespace revisits the postwar dome house—Buckminster Fuller with cedar shingles.

The Zero Carbon House gives an eco-tech twist on the generic suburban model. A gabled box with dormers, it exists everywhere and nowhere at the same time (though it happens to be in Scotland). Of course, if every suburban house were energy neutral, we could worry only about the state of our neighborhoods, not the state of our planet. Accordingly, such projects perfectly demonstrate the status quo of sustainable design—its vision is in the nuts and bolts, not on the napkin sketch.

The high-design equivalent is the Walla Womba Guesthouse, a Tasmanian variation on the Farnsworth, with a bent roof. Passive solar Mies. The influence of the Farnsworth can be seen in the work of another Australian, Glenn Murcutt, which begs a question: How is a 1951 German-designed house in Illinois relevant to contemporary living in Australia? Do the icons of architecture overshadow the particularities of place? The ultimate example of this dilemma is modern prefab, popularized by Michelle Kaufmann's Glide House but epitomized by projects such as Cannatà & Fernandes's "self-sustained module," which feels as much like product design as it does architecture. Stylistic questions aside (prefab is a technique, not a style, though it has made mid-century modern a retro fad), can a project be truly green when it is designed specifically without a site in mind? Can there be such a thing as placeless sustainability?

These questions do not diminish the design of these projects but, rather, underscore the ambition of their aims. Is the modern green home a house with better technology, or is it a whole new way of living? You will find some answers on the following pages.

The symbols on each project's
fact sheet refer to the following:

 ENERGY

 WATER

 MATERIALS

 OTHER

DWELLING IN EL ESCORIAL

Luca Lancini/Fujy   El Escorial, Spain

 Solar photovoltaic - Passive solar - Solar thermal

 Natural materials (partial) - Recycled materials (partial)

 Rainwater collection and use - Blackwater and graywater treatment

Domotics (information and communication technology for the home)

The fruit of participation by universities, public entities, and companies, this project is currently being used as a conference center and exhibition space for products related to sustainable architecture.

The outside walls are made of insulating brick and panels of recycled gypsum board. The front door—made from aluminum with insulated glazing and thermal break—reduces the possibility of heat transfer. A single-layer waterproof finish has been applied to the outside walls in order to further fortify the insulation.

Each exterior wall has been designed to take advantage of climatic factors depending on the season. In the summer, the design makes use of airflow to cool, while in the winter, the sun's rays are harnessed to warm the structure. Likewise, the south wall has a number of systems to guarantee minimum energy consumption: aluminum slats, wood or metalwork with thermal break, greenhouses on the upper level, a solar dryer on the first floor, automatic security blinds, and special glazing to control heat bridging.

The roof is equipped with ecological insulation systems, a pre-finished insulating frame (garage), slate tiling, and automatic ventilation windows to control the natural convection in the greenhouses. Thermal solar panels have also been placed there to produce hot water for the bathrooms and for heating.

Energy is supplied by systems that are passive (greenhouses, slats, electric control grilles and projections) or active (solar thermal collectors), together with supplementary backup from a high-performance furnace. There is also radiant floor heating and cooling, and a gas water cooler. Individual wireless thermostats regulate the temperature in each room.

Photos © Miguel de Guzman

The dwelling occupies forested terrain in El Escorial, a residential area in the northwest of the greater Madrid region.

Location plan

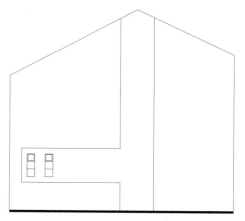

North elevation

South elevation

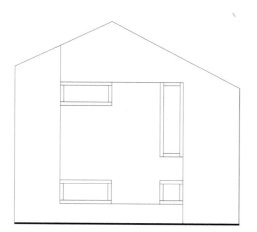

East elevation

West elevation

The interior temperature remains comfortable thanks to hot and cold radiant flooring. An automatic wireless thermostat system regulates the temperature of each room individually.

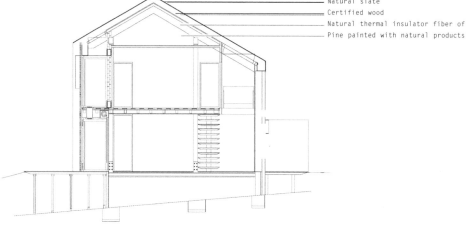

Natural slate
Certified wood
Natural thermal insulator fiber of wood Gutex
Pine painted with natural products

Section 1

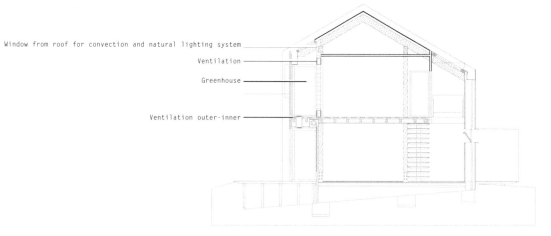

Window from roof for convection and natural lighting system
Ventilation
Greenhouse
Ventilation outer-inner

Section 2

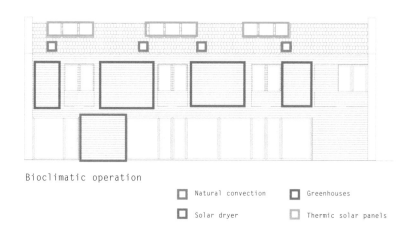

Bioclimatic operation

☐ Natural convection   ☐ Greenhouses
☐ Solar dryer   ☐ Thermic solar panels

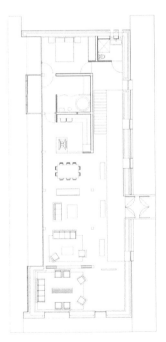

Ground floor

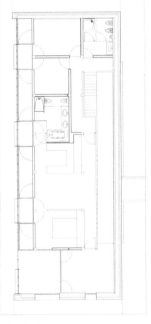

First floor

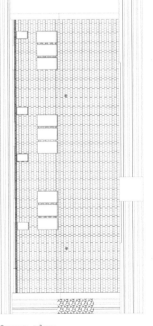

Cover plan

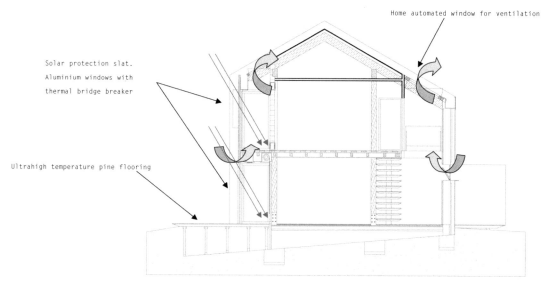

Home automated window for ventilation

Solar protection slat.
Aluminium windows with
thermal bridge breaker

Ultrahigh temperature pine flooring

Bioclimatic section (summer)

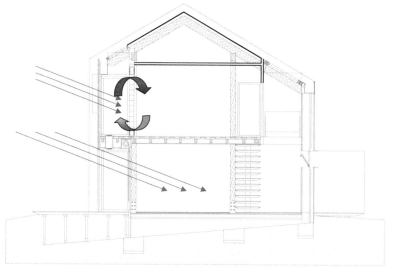

Bioclimatic section (winter)

THE DWIGHT WAY

Leger Wanaselja Architecture   Berkeley, California, U.S.

 Solar photovoltaic

 Natural materials - Reused materials - Recycled materials

Rainwater collection and use

Raw material savings - Native species plantings

Located on one of the busiest corners in Berkeley, the Dwight Way is a living symbol of the marriage of ecological and social expectations in a single project. This nine-unit, mixed-use installation near San Francisco is composed of an existing apartment building, which was remodeled, and a new one. Its ecological design has led to high energy efficiency; also, recycled or salvaged materials with natural finishes were used. As a result, the existing building achieved a 280 percent improvement in energy efficiency, and the new building is now nearly twice as energy efficient as required by local codes.

The chief measures taken to reduce energy consumption include: a) utilizing natural insulation, made from old telephone books and newspapers; b) substituting fly ash for 50 percent of the cement in the concrete; c) leaving the aluminum siding on the second floor of the existing building, instead of replacing it with wood or stucco.

Other measures were taken to reduce the environmental impact of the two structures. Both benefited from: photovoltaic panels; rainwater collection and use; old car parts and street signs reused as railings, awnings, gates, or lighting systems; recycled wood for doors, siding, and walls; FSC-certified wood for framing lumber and flooring; insulating floor slabs; formaldehyde-free kitchen and shower units; non-VOC paints and woodwork finished with natural oils; and native-species plantings.

Photos © Cesar Rubio, Karl Wanaselja

Reused materials of diverse origin form the entrance area to the house, with elements salvaged from street signs used as awnings and dividers.

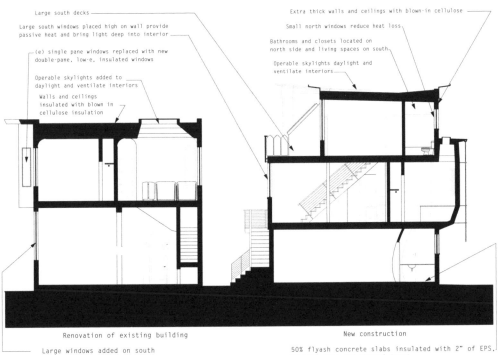

Large south decks

Large south windows placed high on wall provide
passive heat and bring light deep into interior

(e) single pane windows replaced with new
double-pane, low-e, insulated windows

Operable skylights added to
daylight and ventilate interiors

Walls and ceilings
insulated with blown in
cellulose insulation

Extra thick walls and ceilings with blown-in cellulose

Small north windows reduce heat loss

Bathrooms and closets located on
north side and living spaces on south

Operable skylights daylight and
ventilate interiors

Renovation of existing building

Large windows added on south

New construction

50% flyash concrete slabs insulated with 2" of EPS,
tapered edge and thermal break

North south section

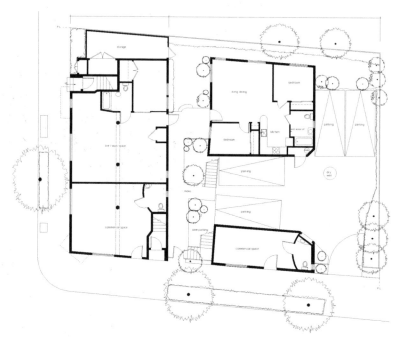

Ground floor and site plans

First and second floor plans

BRUNSELL-SHARPLES HOUSE REMODEL

Obie G. Bowman The Sea Ranch, California, U.S.

 Passive solar - Cross ventilation - Green roof

 Natural materials - Recycled materials

Landscape integration - Adaptation to wind

One of the forces guiding Obie G. Bowman throughout his career has been "a desire to build and a need to work with rather than against the natural landscape".

True to this, the construction of this vacation home and its later remodel in 2005—by the same architect—have sought to minimize any impact on the site's flora and fauna. An example of this is the offsetting of lost meadowland with the creation of a roof garden containing native plant species. The existing topography was taken into account, and the building was integrated into the terrain.

The shape of the dwelling was adapted to the strong winds that are characteristic of the area in the spring and summer. For this reason, the roof was projected up from a low height, offering maximum protection to the southern flank. From there, one can enjoy stunning views of the Pacific Ocean. The reuse and recycling of materials can be seen in the euca-

lyptus-wood timbers that form part of the frame of the dwelling. Also, the brick fireplace was built from unused leftover material salvaged from a brick manufacturer.

Natural aging products or systems were employed on the interiors. Other ecological advantages include the bioclimatic design, which allows the house to take full advantage of both passive solar energy as a natural light source and cross ventilation for cooling during the summer. Rainwater runoff from the roof garden, driveway, and parking area is collected and allowed to seep back into the natural terrain.

The main new structures added as part the remodel were: a sequoia-wood deck at ground level over a concrete floor, and a spa (specially requested by the new owners), which will likely see heavy use. Inside, the bathrooms and the lighting have also been refurbished.

Photos © Obie G. Bowman, Robert Foothorap

The integration of the project into the
landscape is evident in the natural-wood
cladding on the facade.

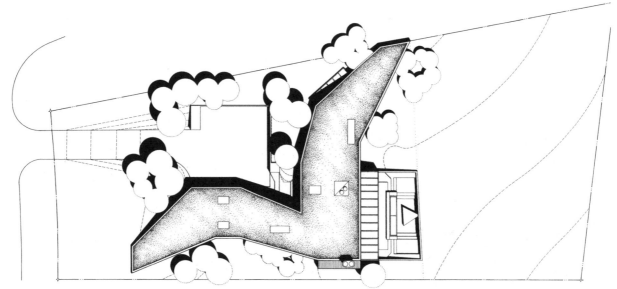

Location plan

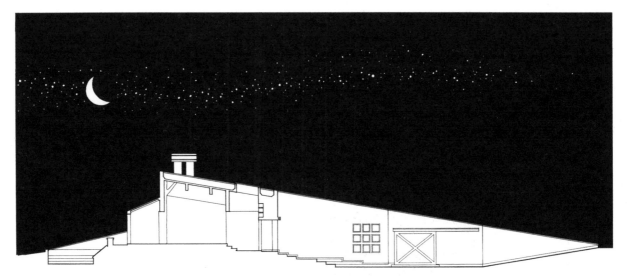

Section

The roof was projected up from a low height to adapt to the strong winds blowing in from the Pacific Ocean and to provide maximum protection to the southern facade.

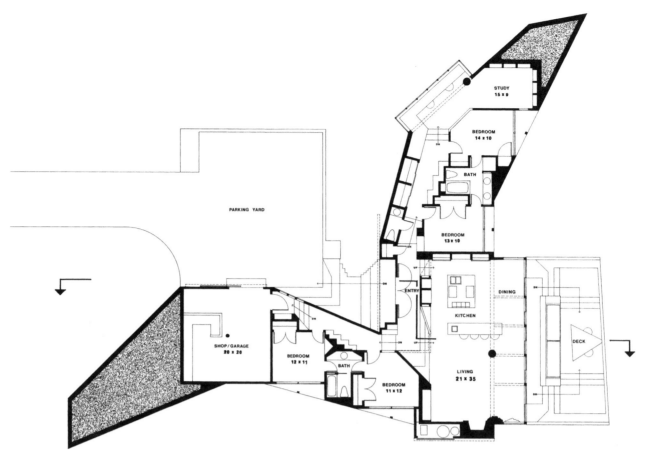

Floor plan

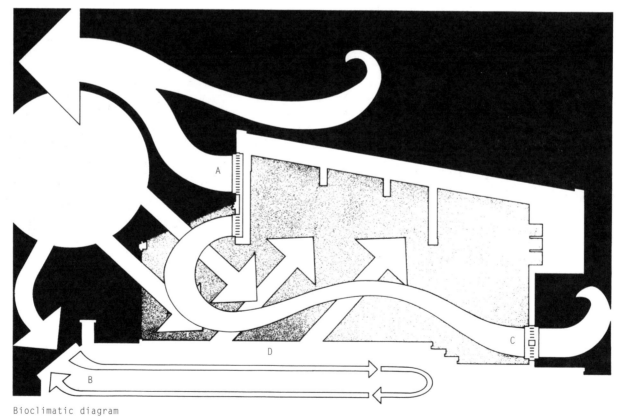

Bioclimatic diagram

A. Continuous discharge manifold
B. Solar hot water collector
C. Air intake louvers
D. Brick over slab floor mass

LES-GWEN MCDONALD HOUSE

Martin Liefhebber / Breathe Architects   Prince Edward County, Canada

 Active solar - Passive solar - Solar thermal - Geothermal - Wind power - Solar chimney - Green roof

 Natural materials

Flying the self-sufficiency flag full mast, this home is not connected to any supply network. Thus, it is considered to be 100 percent self-sufficient in energy.

During the winter months, the majority of the energy needed for heating is from a passive solar system. The space design has taken into account the generation of minimal-size heat sinks (heating loads). Some of the construction strategies employed to ensure self-sufficiency were: a) glazing the south-facing side; b) a compact-volume building style to minimize the surface area; c) thermally broken window frames; d) utilization of the thermal mass of the concrete floor; e) a 3,400-gallon potable hot-water system, using solar thermal panels.

In summer, indoor temperatures are pleasant thanks to the following: a) a chimney effect that evacuates hot air from the upper volume; b) geothermal energy, used to inject 50-degree fresh air inside; c) roof garden thermal regulation.

The electric capacity of the solar thermal collectors is 3,200 kilowatts. The wind turbine supplements these collectors through generating 900 watts of power at a wind speed of 28.6 miles per hour, which is especially important when the weather is cloudy.

The covering used on the facade depends on the direction it faces and its particular use: The south-facing side is made of red-colored wood; the north, which is gray, is built from bales of straw—used as thermal insulation; green-gray fiberglass panels allow natural light to flood the garage.

The concrete floor is fitted with radiant heating. No glue or solvents were used in the finishes, and, as such, the indoor atmosphere is completely VOC free.

Photos © Martin Liefhebber

Translucent fiberglass panels have been placed in the garage area in order to take advantage of direct sunlight and reduce electricity consumption in this area of the dwelling, which usually lacks natural light.

Elevation

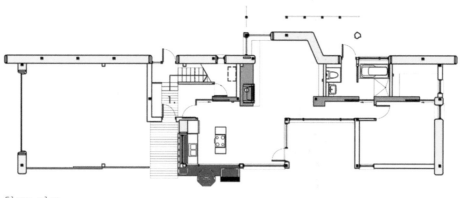

Floor plan

The pale tones of the facade indicate that hay bales have been used in the walls in order to insulate the coldest side of the dwelling.

CAPE SCHANCK HOUSE

Paul Morgan Architects Cape Schanck, Victoria, Australia

 Convection - Cross ventilation

 Native species planting - Adaptation to wind

Rainwater collection and use

Water restrictions, drought, and the risk of bushfires on this stretch of the Australian coast, around 50 miles from Melbourne, were the reason for the architects to design a "water place" in the central area that's normally occupied by living room fireplaces. The house is nestled among tea trees (Melaleuca Alternifolia) for natural protection in a traditionally windy area.

A detailed analysis of dynamic forces—wind energy, turbulence, and phototropism—greatly influenced the design of the dwelling. One of the faces was endowed with an aerodynamic profile so that it could function as a foil against strong winds, while wind scoops on the south wall act as thermal agents, catching cool winds in summer and protecting the house from the sun. At the entrance, the architect decided to bend the wood paneling to suggest the

strong turbulence created when wind tries to enter closed spaces.

The house has no air-conditioning system, so the dwelling's symbolic central bulb is responsible for cool convection air currents and cross ventilation during the summer. It also provides structural support for the roof and serves as a rainwater tank to store water for domestic use (lavatories, washing, and occasionally for drinking).

Concrete flooring, inspired by the pentagonal and hexagonal forms of a nearby rock formation, are a feature of the living room and the terrace. Drought-resistant native plant species were used in the garden.

In short, it is a house that takes its inspiration from the often-parched, rough-and-tumble environs and that prioritizes structural integrity over the ornamental.

Photos © Peter Bennetts

The strength and turbulence of the wind in this part of Australia has marked the central facade of the dwelling, particularly the entrance.

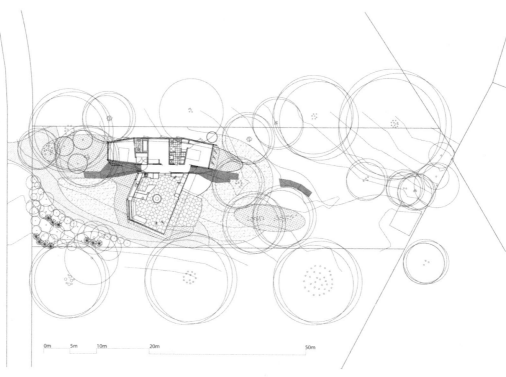

Location plan

0m   5m   10m   20m   50m

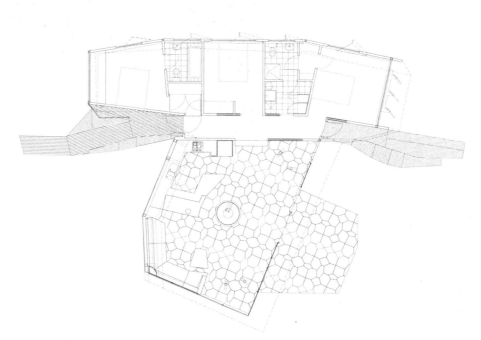

Floor plan

The surrounding tea trees, which lean toward
the sun, are a natural canopy for the dwelling,
protecting it from the unending blast
of strong winds in the area.

The back facade, unlike the front, is hermetically
sealed to the galelike force of the area's winds.

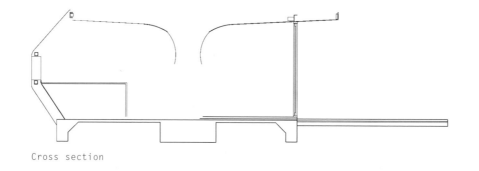

Cross section

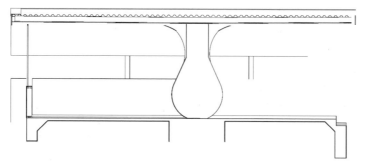

Longitudinal section

SELF-SUSTAINED MODULES

Cannatà & Fernandes Arquitectos   Concreta, Exponor, Oporto, Portugal

 Solar photovoltaic - Solar thermal

 Prefabricated construction - Easy disassembly - Domotics - Construction waste minimized

Both prefabricated modules, for the firms CAPA and DST, were built for presentation at the Spanish construction industry trade fair, Concreta 2003.

The aim was to show alternative solutions to a series of problems related to temporary dwellings, and to demonstrate other possible uses (store, bar, or small fire station).

The components are prefabricated, transported by truck or helicopter, and assembled on site. The architects also considered the possibility of mass-producing this building such that a string of successive modules could create true urban complexes.

The name of the project is self-explanatory in regards to energy consumption. Each module has an independent structure and foundation. Domestic water supply, waste water systems, automated space control, and electricity supply also operate autonomously. Power derives from solar cells, with a photovoltaic panel occupying 194 square feet of the total 291-square-foot roof and a battery storage capacity of three days.

A 132-gallon tank supplies the bathroom and a small kitchen. A vacuum system extracts wastewater.

There are three alternate heating and hot water systems to choose from: a) one element as a backup system to a solar panel; b) a gas hot water heater as a backup system to a solar thermal collector; c) hot water by means of one element and heating thanks to a storage heater connected to a photovoltaic panel.

Reduced construction waste is a feature of prefabricated buildings, and the fact that this house can also be disassembled complements its environmentally friendly character.

Photos © Luis Ferreira Alves

The prefabricated nature of the DST modules
guarantees minimum waste during building and
positioning on the lot.

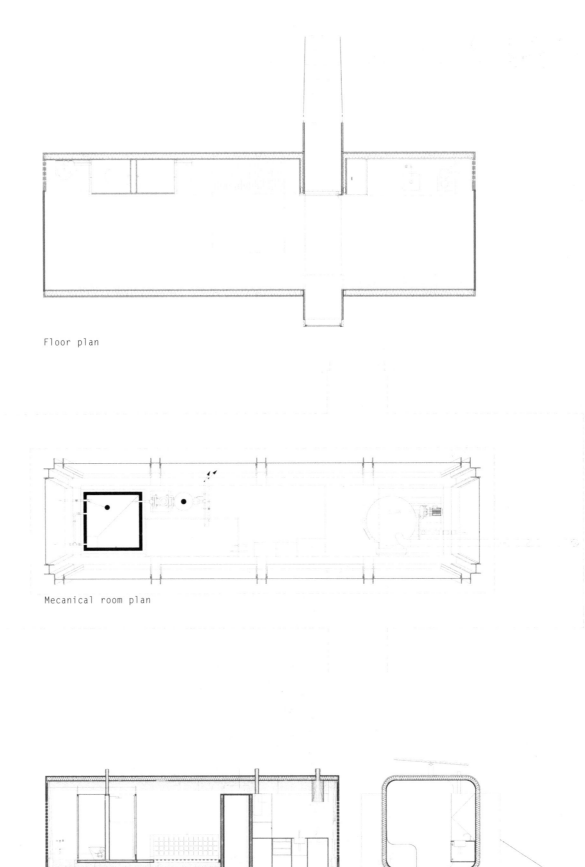

Floor plan

Mecanical room plan

Sections

The ease with which the CAPA module is placed
on-site and its energy self-sufficiency makes
it the equal of a bungalow in terms of space
and mobility.

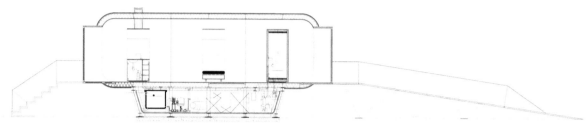

Section

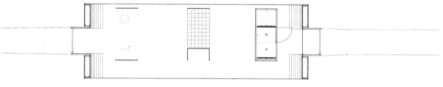

Floor plan

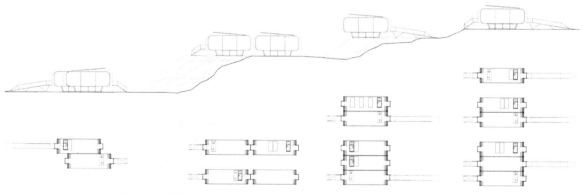

Module combination (elevation/floor plan)

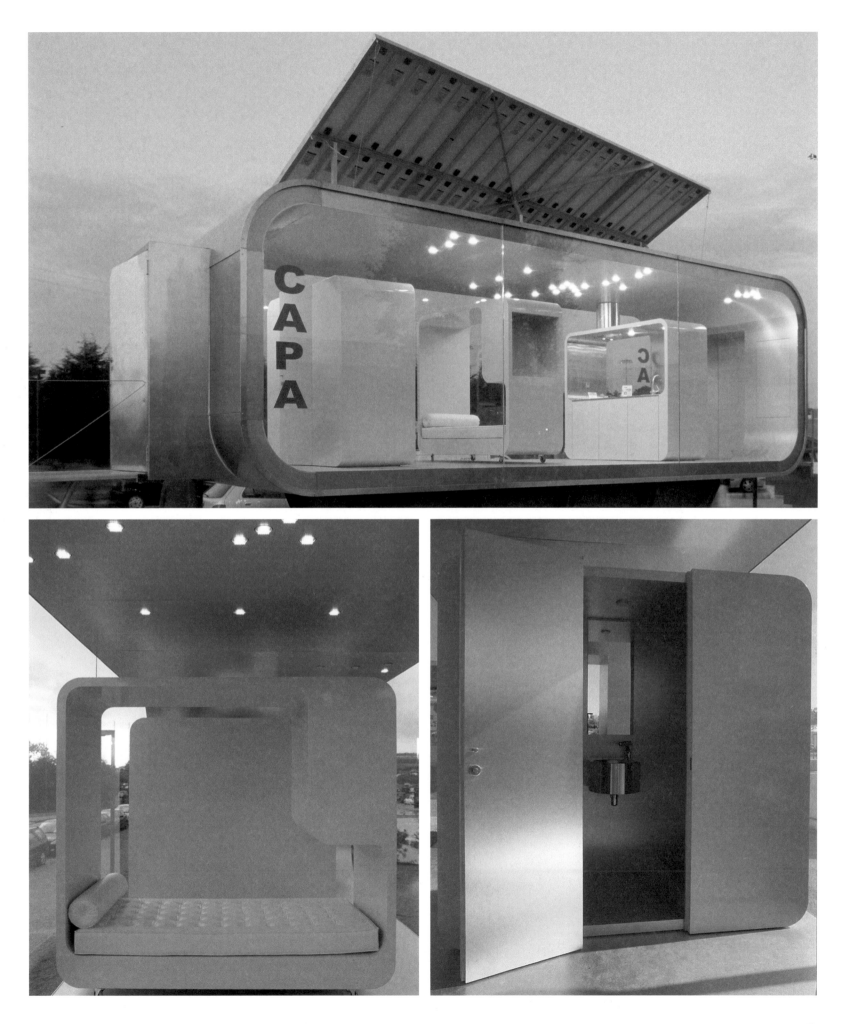

GLIDEHOUSE

Michelle Kaufmann
Novato, California, U.S.

 Solar photovoltaic - Energy efficiency

 Water-saving devices on bathroom fittings

 Natural materials - Recycled materials

Prefabricated construction - Construction waste minimized

Michelle Kaufmann has earned a well deserved North American reputation for prefabricated designs that respect the environment. Her team includes architects certified by Leadership in Energy and Environmental Design (LEED) and members of the U.S. Green Building Council. Her mission: to design and create projects with sustainable materials and techniques, using advanced assembly techniques.

Among the advantages of this modus operandi are: significant reduction in construction waste, long-lasting structures, use of renewable energy (active solar systems), and the ability to achieve a healthy atmosphere for each design built.

The structure and finishes of this dwelling incorporate wood certified by the Forest Stewardship Council (FSC) and ecoresin containing 30 percent recycled ingredients. It features surfaces treated with nontoxic substances, bamboo flooring, and recycled-glass bathroom tiles. Special attention has been given to using low VOC paints.

Icynene, a material certified by the Envirodesic Program for Maximum Indoor Air Quality, serves as the insulation. A mechanical HVAC system ensures comfortable temperatures indoors; it works by circulating outside air through a heat exchanger, then distributing it at high speed and pressure inside to cool or heat the house. The result? Energy use that's about 30 percent that of conventional methods.

Low energy consumption is a pillar of Kaufmann's designs. Using the best available technology, all the components are prefabricated in a factory and assembled on-site, more or less halving the time needed to complete a project. As a result, there is much less waste, and some of this will be reused in the construction cycle of new buildings.

Photos © John Swain

Its prefabricated nature allows construction
time to be halved.

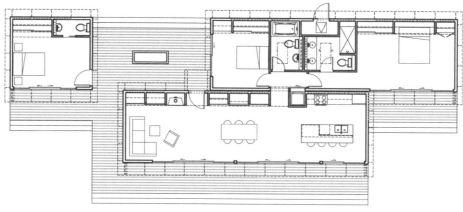

Floor plan

Wooden slats provide an attractive finish
to the outdoor sliding doors, banisters,
and garage facade.

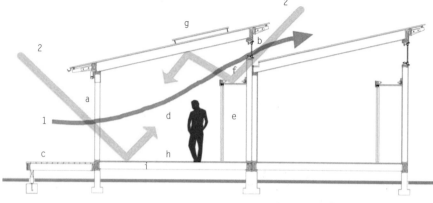

Bioclimatic section

a. Siding-glass-door wall
b. Clerestory windows
c. Outdoor room
d. Indoor living
e. Storage bar with customizable shelving
   behind sliding wooden doors
f. Up-lighting
g. Solar panels on metal standing-seam roofing
h. Bamboo flooring
i. Energy-efficient insulation
1. Cross ventilation in all the main spaces
2. Balanced daylighting-indirect lighting
   washes surfaces with light

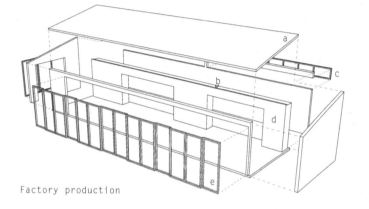

Factory production

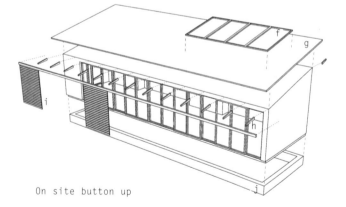

On site button up

a. Roof structure
b. Hidden up-lighting
c. Clerestory windows
d. Storage bar
e. Siding glass wall
f. Site installed solar panels
g. Site installed standing seam metal roofing
h. Roof brackets
i. Siding wood screens
j. Site built foundation
k. Site built deck

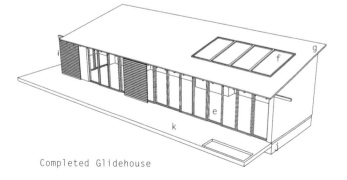

Completed Glidehouse

Diagram

DOMESPACE

Patrick Marsilli Quimper, France

 Passive solar - Cross ventilation

 Natural materials

Organic form - Automatic orientation towards
the sun - Geobiological design

This circular wooden house in the heart of Brittany is currently used as a dwelling and model house. Its creator, Patrick Marsilli, was initially inspired by the sacred architecture of cathedrals and by pyramids. He has built about one hundred of these houses since 1989, mainly in France.

The peculiarity of this building is its ability to rotate in the direction of or contrary to the sun's path. This operation is the precursor of what we know today as domotics, or home automation. Rotation can be done either manually or by remote control, and the house can be turned to the right or left a total of 320 degrees. There is software that automatically adjusts the speed and angle of rotation.

Other features of the design include: resistance to hurricanes and earthquakes, and a large variety of sizes—floor plans of 474 square feet to 2,150 square feet are available.

The advantages of living in this type of structure are evident in the abundant sunlight and the large, central open space, a natural product of the circular shape. The space meets geobiological requirements and is free from electromagnetic disturbances, waterflow, and radioactivity.

Its organic geometry, adapted to a natural setting, resembles the protective shell of an animal or the vernacular structure of the igloo. The frame consists mostly of untreated wood from sustainable (FSC-certified) sources. The roof is made of red cedar, a wood that is extremely resistant to rot. Cork is used for insulation to protect against cold and outside noise while providing good acoustics inside.

During the winter, Domespace makes use of passive solar energy, supplemented by a central fireplace; during the summer, cross ventilation effectively cools the interior.

Photos © Benjamin Thoby

The semisphere-shaped Domespace adapts
perfectly to the lay of the land.

Ground floor

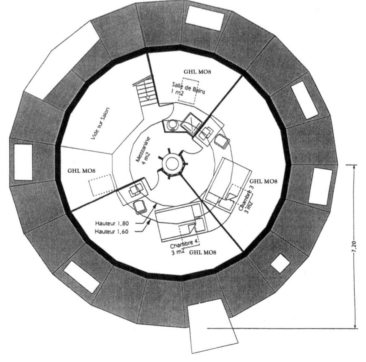

First floor

Although Patrick Marsilli was initially inspired by sacred architecture, his designs also have a notably organic influence.

K & S HOUSE

Jordan   Oed, Austria

 Passive solar

 Recycled materials

The layout of this house was greatly influenced by its location in the northwest section of a residential complex. The Austrian architect specializes in the design of passive solar dwellings, which he defines as houses oriented so that they benefit from the sun during the winter and cross ventilation during the summer.

In this case, he decided to allow the building to face southeast toward the countryside surrounding the site that the house occupies.

The entrance area and the garage are oriented toward the south, not only to face the best of the natural setting, but also to minimize the unattractive view of a warehouse-workshop located across the street.

The exterior walls of the dwelling and roof are clad in wood with cellulose insulation, which is made from pieces of recycled newspaper and compacted in such a way that no draught can enter. This gives very good protection against the summer heat and is good thermal insulation for the winter. In addition, the first floor paving is over rigid-panel insulation. The windows and doors are fabricated from wood and aluminum.

The first floor is where the communal areas, kitchen, expansive living-dining area, and bathrooms are located, while the bedrooms are on the second floor. The garage fits two cars, and the garden is equipped with a shed for tools and other items.

The brightly colored accents on the exteriors contrast with the clean-lined formality of the building.

Photos © Andreas Buchberger

The building occupies the northeastern flank
of the residential complex. Two of its facades
face fields.

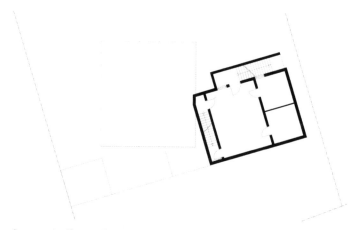

Basement floor plan

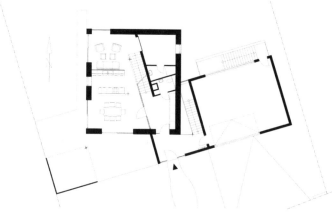

Ground floor plan

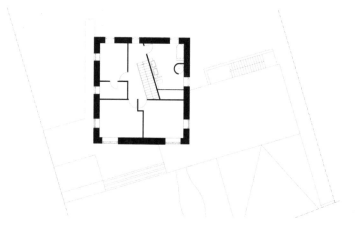

First floor plan

The interiors benefit from the structure's
orientation toward the southwest
to make the best use of sunlight
in both the summer and the winter.

THE SOLAIRE

Pelli Clarke Pelli Architects

New York, New York, U.S.

 Solar photovoltaic - Passive solar

Rainwater collection and use - Graywater treatment

 Natural materials - Recycled materials - Reduced-ecological-footprint building materials

Roof garden - Rubble recycling

The Solaire, which has achieved a gold LEED sustainability rating, is the first green high-rise residential building in the United States. This new twenty-seven-story, brick and glass tower with 293 apartments is located in Battery Park City, a residential and business area adjacent to the site once occupied by the World Trade Center. It is the center-piece of a master plan that also called for the creation of parks and public spaces around the building.

Apartments range from studios to three-bedroom units, all ventilated by a central climate-control system that also humidifies the air in the winter. This system features a four-pipe fan-coil system controlled by digital thermostats.

The building was designed to be 35 percent more energy-efficient than city code requires and to reduce peak power demand by 65 percent. With these goals in mind, natural light now reaches 97 percent of the interior, efficient lighting sys-tems are in place, and some areas (corridors, stairs) are fitted with automatic, sensor-controlled lighting systems. There are photovoltaic panels on some exterior window walls; these produce five percent of the building's energy needs.

Windows that open cover 97 percent of the facade, encour-aging cross ventilation and the proper airing of spaces.

Rainwater is collected and used to water gardens, includ-ing the roof garden. Graywater is fed into an in-building wastewater treatment system, and 55 percent of the total water used in the building is from this system.

Another indicator of the project's environmental cre-dentials is the origin of building materials. Close to 70 per-cent are from sources located within a radius of 497 miles. About 19 percent are recycled materials.

Photos © Jeff Golberg/Esto, Pelli Clarke Pelli Architects, Balmori Associates

MECHANICAL AND ROOF LEVEL
Natural-gas fired absortion HVAC System (no CFCs or HCFCs)
High-efficiency variable speed pumps, motor and fans
Planted roof (irrigated with recycled storm water)
Photovoltaic solar array

EXTERIOR BUILDING MATERIALS AND SYSTEMS
Built-in photovoltaic panels (BIPV) in selected window walls
Reduced air infiltration and enhanced thermal performance
High-performance low-E glass
Regional materials (within 500-mile radius)
Recycled, recyclable, or sustainable materials

SET-BACK ROOF LEVEL
Landscaped roof garden (irrigated with recycled storm water)
High albedo roofing materials

Environmentally sustainable features (exterior)

GROUND AND BASEMENT LEVELS
Provisions for future fuel cell
Enhanced day lighting
Energy-efficient lighting with daylight sensors
Basement level
Water recycling plant
Storm-water storage tank for site irrigation
Parking garage with efficient lighting, and carbon monoxide detection and monitoring
Secure bicycle parking

INTERIOR BUILDING MATERIALS AND SYSTEMS
Chlorine-free insulation
Low or no VOC materials
Commissioning and air-quality monitoring
Computerized building management systems
Recycled, recyclable, or sustainable materials
Centralized, filtered, and conditioned central air supply
Energy-efficient corridor and stair lighting with occupancy sensors
Regional materials (within 500-mile radius)

TYPICAL APARTMENTS
Central filtered and conditioned air supply, including humidification during winter months
Four-pipe fan-coil system providing year-round heating or cooling, digital thermostats, quiet operation, and high-efficiency air filtration
Master electrical shutoff with efficient lighting and Energy Star efficient appliances
Low-flow plumbing fixtures

Environmentally sustainable features (interior)

This residential tower shines as an exemplar of sustainable building on the Manhattan skyline.

Location plan

Green roof

Wall comparison (Axonometric projection)

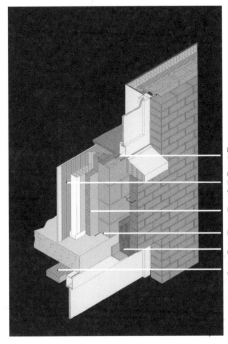

Windows sealed on both
interior and exterior sides

Continuous vapor barrier
sealed to floor, ceiling
and windows

Rigid insulation

Block sealed to structure

Flashing attached to continuous
metal closure sealant

Rigid insulation at
window-head closure

BPC 18A Wall

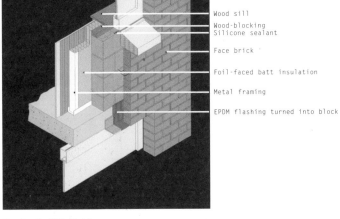

GWB
CMU Block

Thermally broken aluminium frame

Insulated low-E glass

Wood sill
Wood-blocking
Silicone sealant

Face brick

Foil-faced batt insulation

Metal framing

EPDM flashing turned into block

Typical NYC Wall

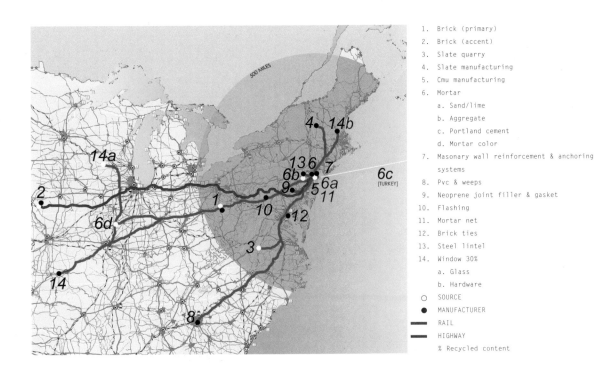

Materials source distance/transport

1.	Brick (primary)	10%
2.	Brick (accent)	
3.	Slate quarry	
4.	Slate manufacturing	
5.	Cmu manufacturing	25%
6.	Mortar	
	a. Sand/lime	
	b. Aggregate	
	c. Portland cement	
	d. Mortar color	
7.	Masonary wall reinforcement & anchoring	
	systems	50%
8.	Pvc & weeps	100%
9.	Neoprene joint filler & gasket	
10.	Flashing	
11.	Mortar net	100%
12.	Brick ties	50%
13.	Steel lintel	50%
14.	Window 30%	
	a. Glass	23%
	b. Hardware	85%
○	SOURCE	
●	MANUFACTURER	
▬	RAIL	
▬	HIGHWAY	
	% Recycled content	

SEATRAIN HOUSE

Jennifer Siegal — Los Angeles, California, U.S.

 Reused materials

Modular construction - Easy disassembly - Raw material savings - Construction waste minimized

A clear example of post-industrial architecture, Seatrain House is located in the Brewery, a district of downtown Los Angeles that is home to a community of 300 lofts used as artists' workshops and residences. In Seatrain, the designer has made use of industrial containers and local steel to provide a fast and alternative solution to housing problems. This system is a paradigm of sustainable construction and is starting to become commonplace in cities like London and Amsterdam, where rising housing prices have encouraged seeking out low-cost, sustainable solutions.

The industrial landscape of the Brewery has heavily influenced Seatrain's design, and it makes good use of commercial and industrial materials. These materials were not salvaged for practical or economic reasons, but to create, in the architect's words, "a unique, dramatic architectural vocabulary."

It took about fifteen days to put up the frame and two months to finish the project. Despite incorporating energy-saving construction processes, the dwelling is not energy self-sufficient—it is connected to the local power grid.

The frame is two ISO shipping containers joined together and two grain trailers that act as a small pond and a lap pool. A roof of sheet steel and glass protects the house itself.

The positioning of the containers together gives a total living space of about 3,000 square feet and explains their modular configuration. Spaces such as the library, dining room, and office can be combined on the first floor. The bedroom is upstairs and enjoys the best views.

The modular frame has a sculptural and practical versatility that allows a great diversity of forms. If need be, the house can even be moved to a new location.

Despite the industrial setting of the Brewery, the architect managed to make a recycled dwelling with an enviable garden compatible with inner-city Los Angeles.

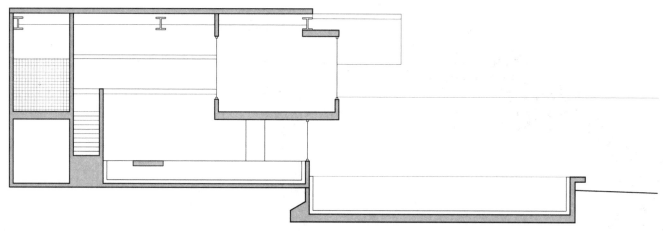

Section

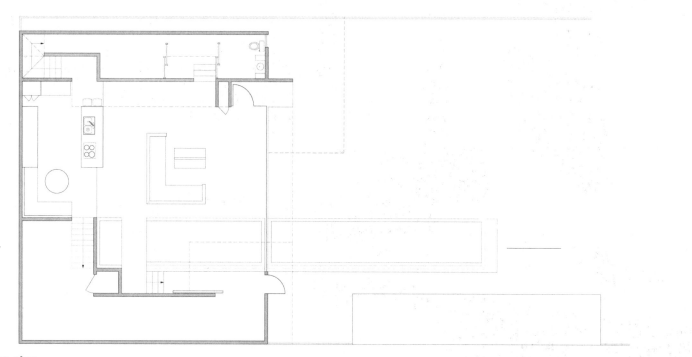

Floor plan

The modular floor plan gives residents
the room to lay out spaces at will.

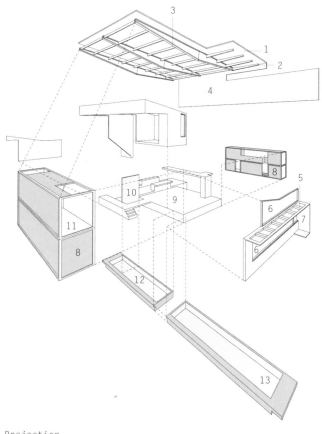

Projection

1. B-36 steel roof decking
2. Tapered steel beams
3. Recycled-wood joists
4. Plate-steel security wall
5. Tube-steel pergola
6. Aluminum-frame windows
7. Salvage-steel cladding
8. Seatrain storage containers
9. Cherrywood flooring
10. Flagstone water wall
11. Recycled carpet
12. Aluminum grain-trailer koi pond
13. Aluminum grain-trailer lap pool

BETWEEN ALDER AND OAK

Andreas Wenning/Baumraum   Bad Rothenfelde, Germany

 Natural materials

 Easy disassembly - Recyclable

Tree houses are fragile structures supported by living beings (in this case, an oak tree reinforced with two oblique wooden posts), which means that the useful life of one depends to a large extent on the strength and life of the tree it is built in.

The name of the project simply responds to the fact that the tree house is built between two different species of tree: an alder and an oak. Built for a family with grown-up children and located near Osnabrück in northern Germany, this wooden cabin—five meters above the ground—provides its residents with a space for rest and relaxation, and the possibility of adapting one of the compartments for use as a guest room.

The oak that partially supports the load was not strong enough, so the architect placed two support posts over a concrete base for security. At the height of four meters, there is a platform-terrace with a table and a few chairs, and an upper cabin with a curved roof clad in wood and bitumen. A few steps lead up from the terrace to the cabin.

Oak is the predominant building material. The railings that limit the habitable space are made of oak and steel. The side walls are covered in oak panels over rockwool, which serves as both insulation and wind foil.

From inside the cabin, thanks to wall-spanning windows and a skylight, the occupants can freely enjoy nature, which is literally within their grasp.

Photos © Alasdair Jardine

The dream of living in and with nature comes
true in this type of home, which puts
most of its weight on the resilient oak trunk.

Cross elevation

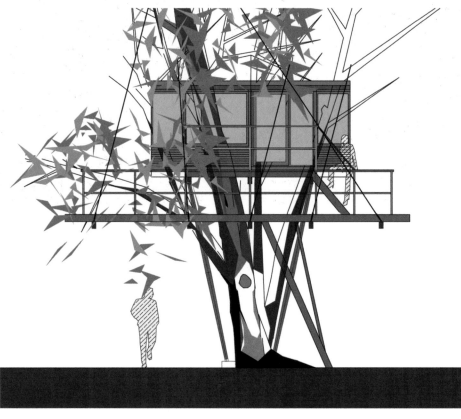

Longitudinal elevation

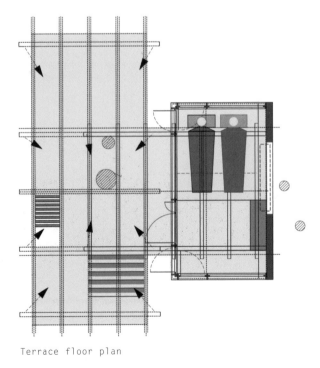

Terrace floor plan

LOBLOLLY HOUSE

Kieran Timberlake Associates   Taylors Island, Maryland, U.S.

 Passive solar - Green roof

 Prefabricated construction - Easy disassembly - Construction waste minimization

Natural materials - Raw material savings

Situated on Taylors Island off the coast of Maryland, this residence makes use of its privileged location—close to Chesapeake Bay and flanked by a small grove of loblolly pines—to enhance its sustainable construction features.

The house is built on a platform raised two meters above the ground on piles of loblolly pine, leaving the area underneath mainly as parking space.

The entire dwelling was assembled on-site, including the floor and ceiling panels in a period of some six weeks. Its prefabricated interior finishes include fiber-cement panels, cedar wood, and birch plywood paneling. An aluminum scaffold served as the structural frame and the means for connecting radiant floor heating, potable water, wastewater, ventilation, and electrical systems. This type of building design gives significant energy savings, inherent in pre-fabricated architecture, plus savings in raw materials and construction time. A roof garden provides natural cooling during the summer and insulates the structure during the winter. Raising the dwelling above the ground protects it from the damp terrain.

The system operating the hangar doors on the main wall also makes the most of winter solar radiation and allows breezes to enter and circulate during the summer months.

A small ground-level garden of bamboo, capable of growing as high as the roof thanks to a semiopen atrium, serves as a unifying note of harmony to a project that is in tune with the environment.

The home's structural versatility is justified by the little time needed for its disassembly. Instead of waste and debris, it leaves whole parts that can be reclaimed.

Photos © Barry Halkin

The prefabricated and fragmented cladding of
three of the walls is made of cedar planks.

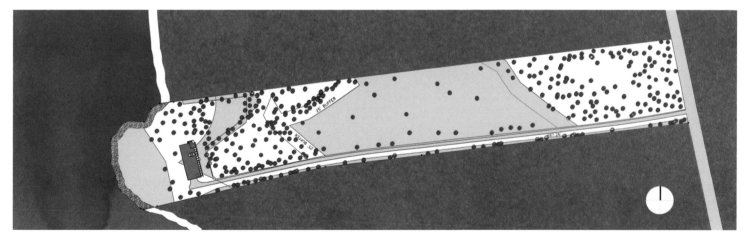

Location plan

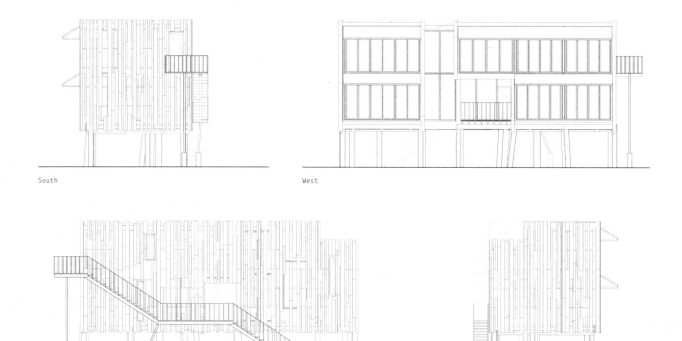

South

West

East

North

Elevations

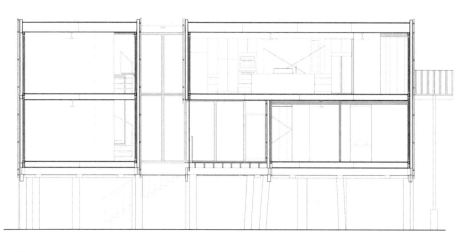

Section

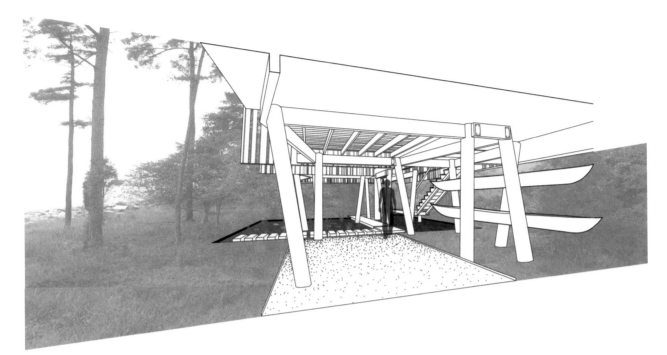

View under house

North view

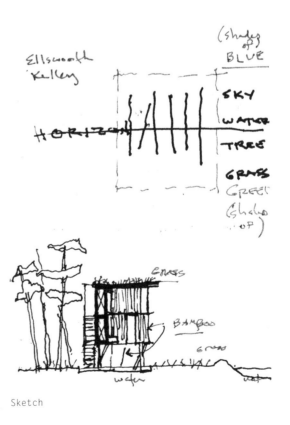

Sketch

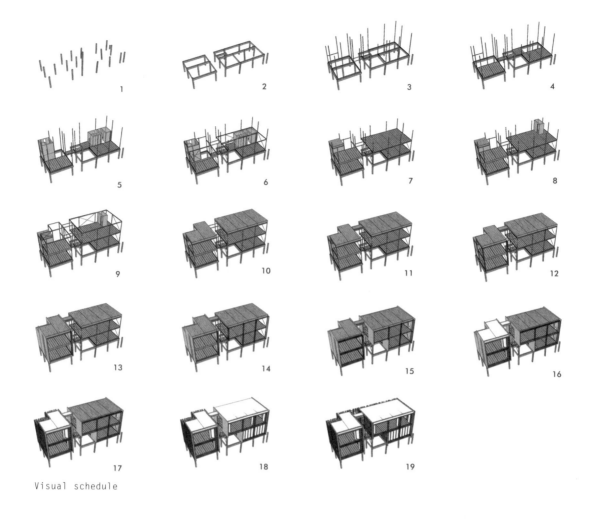

Visual schedule

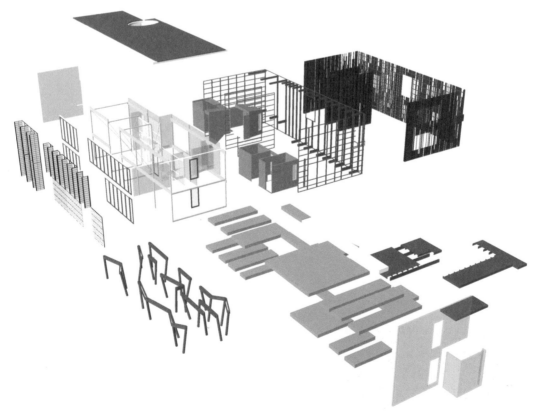

Prefab elements

Bioclimatic schemes

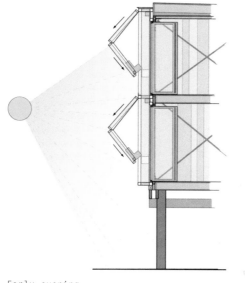

Early evening

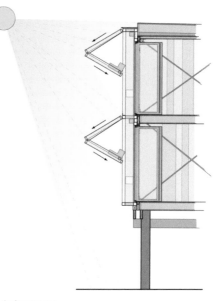

Midafternoon

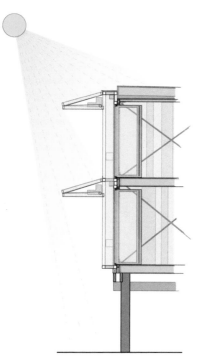

Noon

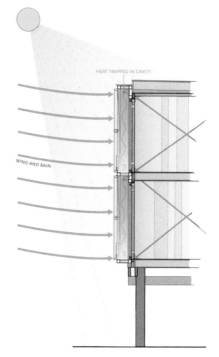

Protection from wind and rain
provides solar insulation

First Floor Plan

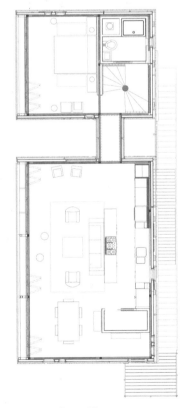

Second Floor Plan

WALLA WOMBA GUESTHOUSE

1+2 Architecture   Bruny Island, Tasmania, Australia

 Solar photovoltaic - Passive solar

 Wastewater purification - Landscape integration

Rainwater collection and use

Located on an island of Tasmania, this modernist residence, made of two parallel wings joined by a glass corridor, typifies a refuge in the heart of nature. The remote place, set amongst tall windswept trees and bushland, elicits maximum respect for its rugged beauty.

As a consequence, the architect chose to build on an elevated steel frame, reducing the risk and impact that excavation would have on native vegetation.

The materials used in its construction, the finishes, and exterior colors were chosen as a reflection of the house's setting. Steel was used for the frame; wood and corrugated steel, as wall cladding; and corrugated galvanized iron, for the roof. An attempt was made to reproduce the tones from the surrounding landscape.

The house is laid out on an east-west axis, endowing it with the full advantage of the sun's movement and corresponding energy efficiency. The floor plan was designed in relation to the position of the sun, and to benefit from cross ventilation. Care was taken to ensure quality insulation, and glazing was also used. Where passive solar energy is not enough, photovoltaic panels and a supplementary generator satisfy the house's energy requirements.

The guesthouse is not connected to any local water supply systems or sewage network. Instead, rainwater is collected for domestic use, and wastewater from the bathrooms is gathered in a septic tank. The contents of this tank are filtered, and the water is treated by the very bacteria it contains.

Photos © 1 + 2 Architecture, Peter Hyatt

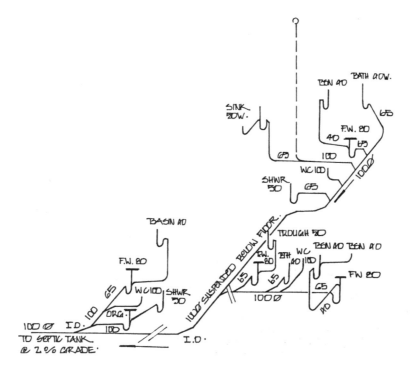

Sanitary plumbing isometric

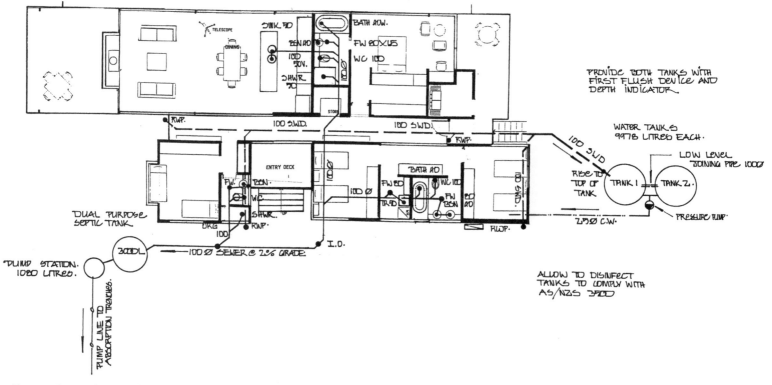

Storm water and sewer drainage

A refuge in the heart of nature not connected
to drinking water, power, or sewerage networks.

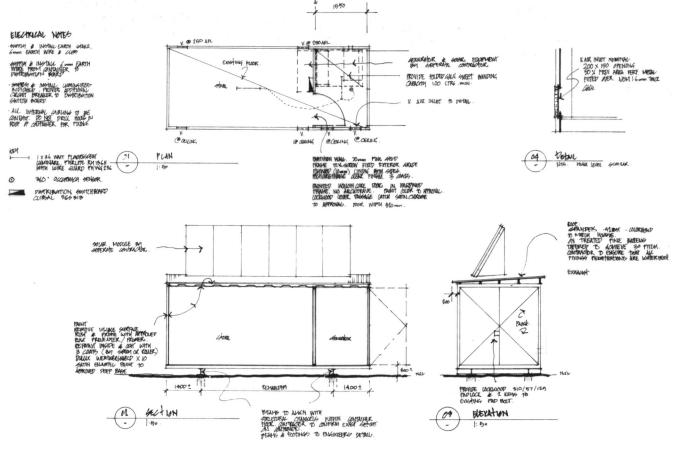

Solar and generator electrical system

Z6 HOUSE

Ray Kappe   Santa Monica, California, U.S.

 Solar photovoltaic - Solar thermal - Cross ventilation - Green roof

Graywater reuse - Rainwater collection and use - Drought-resistant plant species

 Natural or partially natural materials

Prefabricated construction - Good connections

LivingHomes is a premier residential developer that works with world-class architects to create modern, prefabricated, and sustainable homes. The first built model is the Z6 house, a two-story, 2,480-square-foot residence in Santa Monica, California. It was conceived as a "infill, move-up, and second-home venue". In August 2006, the Z6 became the first residential project to win a Platinum LEED rating, the highest possible from the U.S. Green Building Council's new LEED for Homes rating system.

The ecological achievements of the Z6 comprise: the site (low environmental impact on the location and erosion control during construction); drought-resistant ground cover (species in the garden and on the green roof are native); the use of wastewater or rainwater (graywater reuse, rainwater collection); and energy efficiency (solar, thermal, and photovoltaic panels; natural ventilation; use of LEDs for lighting; and general design).

The architects also factored in: (1) eco-efficient use of raw materials (wood as pure embellishment is prohibited; use of FSC-certified wood); (2) the high quality of the interior air (air is filtered as it passes through the house, and humidity buildup is reduced with a corresponding improvement in material maintenance); and (3) use of natural building materials (insulation containing part cellulose from old paper, and wood pulp in cement slabs; use of paint and primers without preservatives, fungicides, and low VOC content).

The result is a family home that retains the clean lines of its core, remains well-ventilated, and boasts easy access to the nearby business district, beach, or public transit by foot or by bicycle.

Photos © CJ Berg

The modular construction offers the chance to
create a breathing, well-ventilated space.

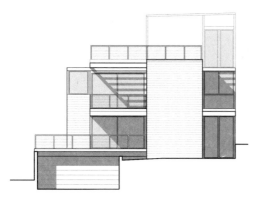

East elevation

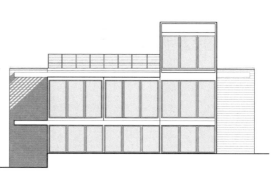

North elevation

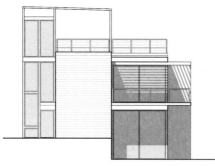

West elevation

South elevation

Ground floor

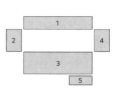

First floor

1. Kitchen
2. Entry/gallery
3. Living area
4. Dining
5. Study
6. Powder room
7. Laundry/pantry
8. Media
9. Upper living
10. Master bed
11. Master bath
12. Bedroom
13. Guest bed

The clerestory atop the roof of the
dwelling provides cross ventilation and
effective temperature control of the interior.

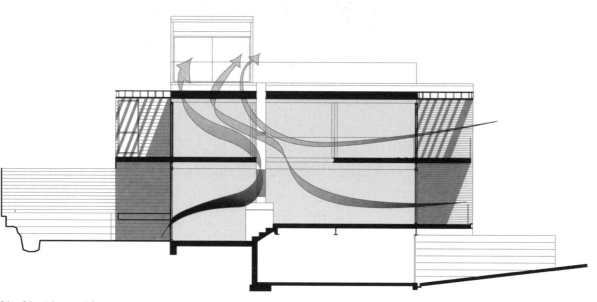

Bioclimatic section

F10 HOUSE

Chicago, Illinois, U.S.

 Passive solar - Solar chimney - Cross ventilation - Green roof

 Construction waste minimization

Natural materials - Reused materials

EHDD won the Green Homes for Chicago competition for the design of this dwelling. Then the Chicago Departments of Housing and Environment commissioned the firm to build it. The architects' mission? Maximum energy savings and maximum reduction in materials.

So the designers strove to minimize life-cycle environmental impacts by a factor of ten compared to the average home built in America at the beginning of the millennium. Consequently, size was reduced as much as possible, and the impact on the site was calculated from the time of construction.

The result was a space of 1,830 square feet squeezed into the Chicago inner city. It was the antithesis of the enormous homes being erected in the suburbs. The narrow footprint belies an expansive, white-walled, open-plan interior. As for energy consumption of the dwelling during its useful life, the main work is carried out by a solar chimney in the stairwell, with bioclimatic advantages, particularly in the summer, when it draws out warm air that builds up at the top of the house. A design feature that produces such cross ventilation makes air-conditioning unnecessary.

During the winter, the opposite effect is achieved. A fan in the middle of the ceiling helps to pull warm air into the building through the clerestory. A sculptural wall of full water bottles acts as a heat sink, storing up the sun's warmth during the day and releasing it at night. Complementing this, the windows face south to capture sunlight for as many hours as possible.

The exterior is clad in red-stained fiber-cement siding, and the insulation consists mainly of cellulose. A garden is planted on the roof, with all the energy-saving advantages this brings.

Photos © Doug Snower

EHDD chose reduced proportions for their building to reduce the need for building materials and the generation of waste.

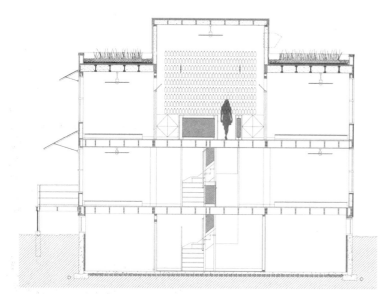

Longitudinal section

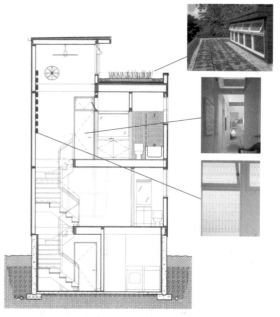

Cross section

The clerestory and the herb garden on the roof
play important roles in controlling the
temperature inside the dwelling in all seasons.

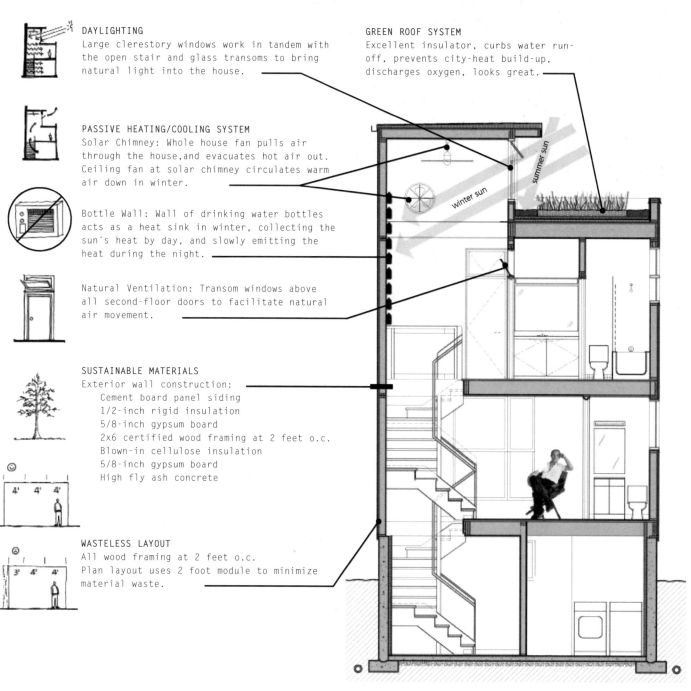

DAYLIGHTING
Large clerestory windows work in tandem with the open stair and glass transoms to bring natural light into the house.

GREEN ROOF SYSTEM
Excellent insulator, curbs water run-off, prevents city-heat build-up, discharges oxygen, looks great.

PASSIVE HEATING/COOLING SYSTEM
Solar Chimney: Whole house fan pulls air through the house,and evacuates hot air out. Ceiling fan at solar chimney circulates warm air down in winter.

Bottle Wall: Wall of drinking water bottles acts as a heat sink in winter, collecting the sun's heat by day, and slowly emitting the heat during the night.

Natural Ventilation: Transom windows above all second-floor doors to facilitate natural air movement.

SUSTAINABLE MATERIALS
Exterior wall construction:
　　Cement board panel siding
　　1/2-inch rigid insulation
　　5/8-inch gypsum board
　　2x6 certified wood framing at 2 feet o.c.
　　Blown-in cellulose insulation
　　5/8-inch gypsum board
　　High fly ash concrete

WASTELESS LAYOUT
All wood framing at 2 feet o.c.
Plan layout uses 2 foot module to minimize material waste.

winter sun

summer sun

Bioclimatic section

Marginal diagrams: Schoolyards to Skylines, copyright Chicago Architectural Foundation 2002. Used with permission.

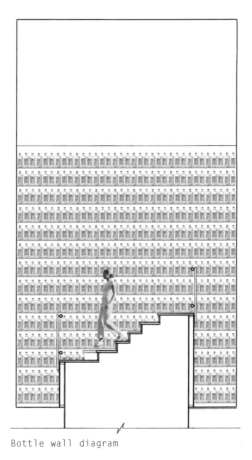

Bottle wall diagram

HOUSE W

Markus Gentner/att architekten · Gräfenberg, Germany

 Biomass - Cross ventilation

Rainwater collection and use - Blackwater and graywater treatment

 Natural materials

Respect for traditional local building styles

This property of nearly half an acre is located in Bavaria's Franconia region, also known as Franconian Switzerland. The architect has attempted to respect the traditional building style of the area, a combination of living areas and workshops joined in compositions of rectangular structures with simple gabled roofs.

House W is based on this Franconia farmhouse vernacular. Using that as a starting point, the various living areas were restructured. An existing cherry tree was preserved, and the central courtyard was laid out around it.

The core is occupied by an auxiliary structure (garage and heating system with a biomass-fed furnace); a single-floor public living space for cooking, dining, working, and entertainment; and a two-story building with sleeping quarters. An articulated entrance connects the three buildings.

The frame of each building is a reinterpretation of the region's traditional *Frankisch* architecture: A classic pitched roof stands out as the main element of the cubelike structure, the facade details are kept to a minimum, and natural materials prevail.

The dwelling needs little energy for climate control: Simple ventilation is enough during the summer, and winter heating for the various rooms is achieved with a renewable resource—biomass combustion using pellets.

Rainwater is collected in a cistern and used for the washing machine, sanitary fixtures, and garden. Little pavement is present outside, which allows natural rainwater seepage. Wastewater is not taken out via sewerage, but is removed to a microbiological treatment system. It is treated there and left to seep into the surrounding terrain.

Photos © Stefan Meyer

The buildings are a clear reference to the
traditional rural *Frankisch* building style
of this part of Germany.

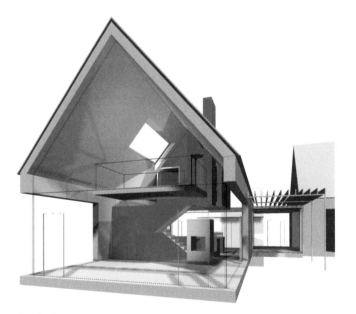

Rendering

Model house

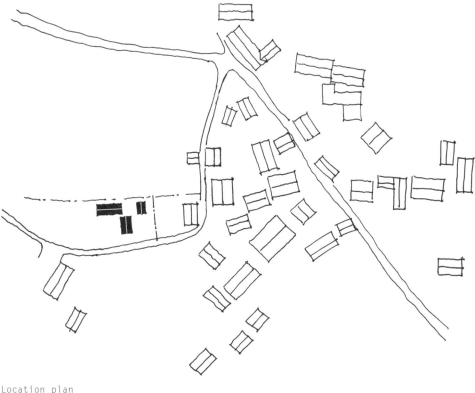

Location plan

South elevation

Ground floor

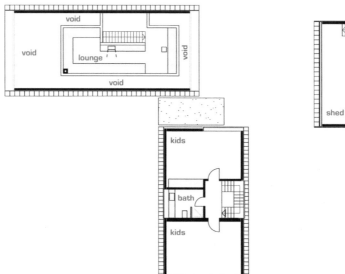

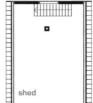

First floor

LEBLANC HOUSE

Peter Cardew Architects — West Vancouver, Canada

 Passive solar

Remodeling - Respect for traditional local building styles

Durability of materials

The essence of this project was to retain the past to sustain the future. This was the basis for Peter Cardew Architects' remodel of a sprawling, aging house under threat of demolition. It allowed the designers to achieve their goals: important savings in materials and energy, and extending the useful life of the structure.

The Leblanc House inherited the typical postwar split-level architecture style—a style that, in Canada, has never been accorded sufficient importance to make preservation of such buildings a priority and, thus, prevent their demolition. As such, it is up to the client and the architect to decide in favor of preserving this typical mid-1950s national building style. The cultural value of such conservation is above and beyond financial benefit. This renovation is not merely the simple preservation of a example from the most important Canadian housing boom, it also shows how an existing structure can be adapted to respond to modern-day needs.

Staying true to this approach, designers were not concerned with slashing construction time. Instead, they emphasized contracting local specialists to work with everyday materials. This essentially traditional approach led to minimal structural changes; the few that were carried out were aimed at improving efficiency and durability. In the process, many existing materials were not wasted.

The renovation materials were chosen for their durability and reflectivity, the latter being used to give the house a glowing appearance. The main changes included installing more efficient windows and an in-floor radiant heating system, and making improvements to the insulation.

Photos © Peter Cardew, Sarah Murray

One of the most important changes of the
remodelling project was the installation of
efficient radiant floor heating.

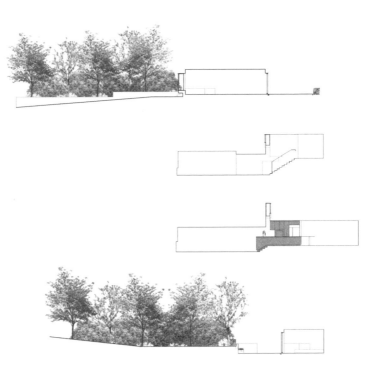

Sections

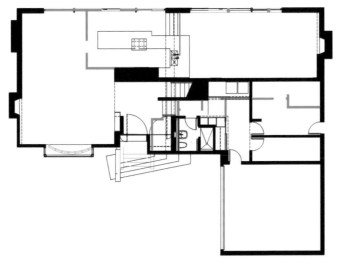

Before/after floor plans

Before/after

First floor
(new configuration)

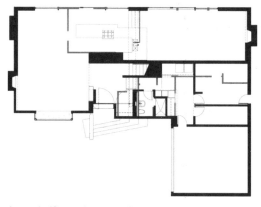

Ground floor (new configuration)

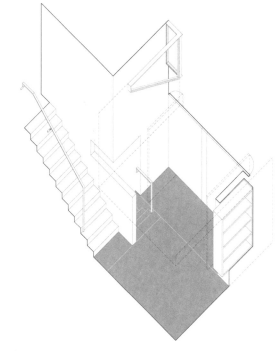

Stair diagram

EASTERN SIERRA RESIDENCE

Arkin Tilt Architects   Gardnerville, Nevada, U.S.

 Solar photovoltaic - Passive solar - Green roof

 Raw material savings

Natural materials - Reused materials - Recycled materials

To a large extent, the architectural design of this residence responds to its mountain setting and the harsh climatic conditions of the area. Located on an eastern slope of the Sierra Nevadas, the dwelling is laid out eco-efficiently around a shaded garden, protected from the summer heat and the winter winds.

The building is energy self-sufficient thanks to the use of solar technology. On a passive level, where and how to make use of shade was taken into account, and efficient insulation and a sod roof help to prevent overheating in the summer. On an active level, photovoltaic panels produce electricity, solar thermal panels provide hot water, and radiant floor heats the house.

Load-bearing walls are made from straw bales with an earthen finish (the soil was taken from the site) with slatted cement-board siding over them. Reused and recycled materials are in many parts of the house: (a) the greenhouses are fitted with airplane flaps as sunshades; (b) the kitchen counters are fabricated from salvaged glass; (c) beams used on the first floor were taken from an aircraft hangar; and (d) the first-floor ceiling was pieced together with vinegar-barrel lids.

Visually blending in completely with the setting, the dwelling is organized into different volumes, giving it a fragmented character, enhanced by the amalgam of materials used and by its formal layout.

Photos © Edward Caldwell

The green roofs, besides insulating the dwelling,
offer a natural habitat for plants and animals.

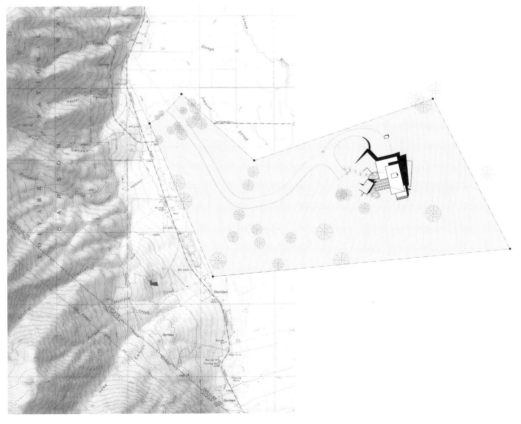

Location plan

Ground floor

First floor

Basement floor

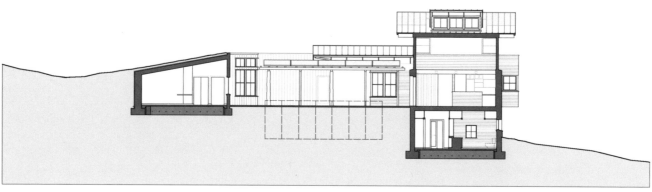

Section

A general view of the house shows its
articulated, uneven look, and its adaptation
to the colors of its natural setting.

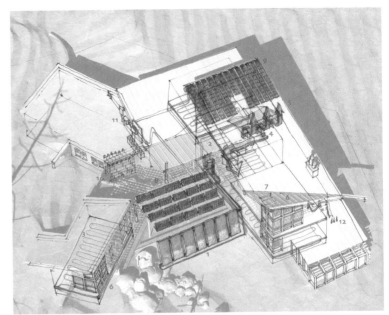

1. Solar hot water collectors
2. Heat exchange for dom.hot water
3. Thermal storage sand bed
4. Night flush cooling
5. High clerestory ventilation
6. Passive solar heat gain
7. Glass floor tiles for daylight
8. PV array shades terrace
9. Roof integrated PV laminates
10. Trombe wall warms batteries
11. Inverters connect to grid
12. Greenhouse adds humidity

Bioclimatic features

EHRLICH RESIDENCE

John Friedman Alice Kimm Architects
Santa Monica, California, U.S.

 Solar photovoltaic - Passive solar - Convection -
Thermal mass - Solar chimney

 Natural materials

The design objective of this 3,900-square-foot dwelling is clear from its very layout: to generate a continuous space, making the most of natural light and creating a close relationship between interior and exterior. Its residents already had a clear idea that they wanted to take full advantage of the south facade in order to boost sunlight penetration in the winter and to provide cross ventilation during the summer. They also requested that living spaces open onto the garden.

The resulting floor plan reveals an L-shaped building around the garage opening onto a garden that is likewise L-shaped. The house is clad mainly with plaster and cement board, both in natural tones. The wood used for the main door, on the stairs, and on the second floor is from a sustainably managed forest.

On the southwest elevation, the overhanging eaves block the summer sun but allow the winter sun to heat up the floor, which is constructed of concrete—a material known for its capacity as a thermal mass. There is also a complementary in-floor radiant heating system.

The house does not have an air-conditioning system, and the reflecting pool cools the rooms surrounding it in the summer by means of breeze convection. The atrium containing the stair acts as a solar chimney in the summer by venting hot air from the house through a pair of motorized skylights in the roof and drawing in cool air.

The dwelling also features a 4 kilowatt photovoltaic system that provides about 85 percent of the energy that the house normally needs.

Photos © Benny Chan/Fotoworks

The pond in the garden cools the house thanks
to air convection created through by water
evaporation.

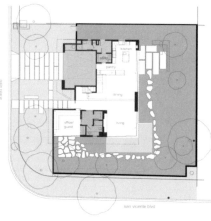

Ground floor

First floor

Roof plan

The owners wanted to highlight the strong
relationship between interior and exterior. The
house looks out over the garden and benefits
fully from abundant direct sunlight.

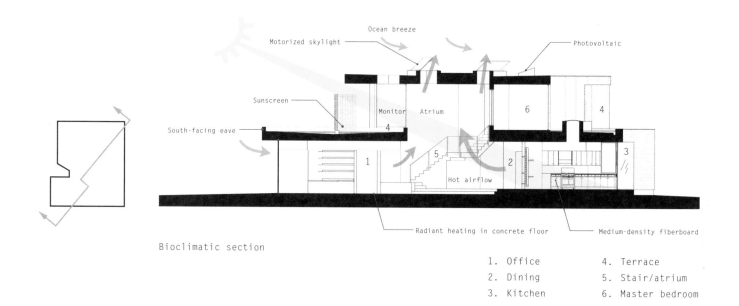

Bioclimatic section

1. Office
2. Dining
3. Kitchen
4. Terrace
5. Stair/atrium
6. Master bedroom

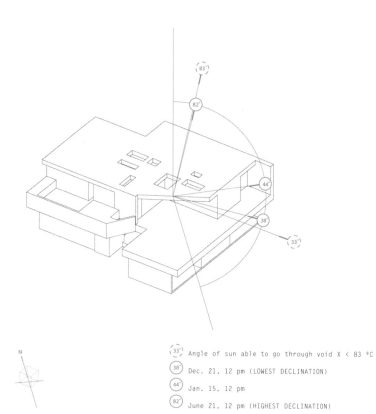

Sun analysis diagram

(33°) Angle of sun able to go through void X < 83 °C
(38°) Dec. 21, 12 pm (LOWEST DECLINATION)
(44°) Jan. 15, 12 pm
(82°) June 21, 12 pm (HIGHEST DECLINATION)

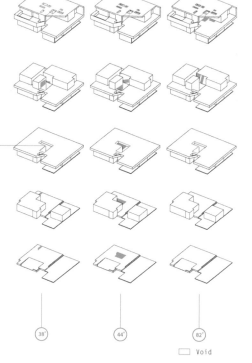

38° 44° 82°

☐ Void
▨ Sun fall-off area

LLIRI BLAU RESIDENTIAL COMPLEX

Luis de Garrido   Massalfassar, Valencia, Spain

 Passive solar - Solar thermal - Green roof

 Rainwater collection and use

 Natural materials - Reused materials - Recycled materials

Partially prefabricated construction - Domotics - Construction waste minimized

This residential complex of highly energy-efficient dwellings is one of the first of its kind built in Spain. It consists of 129 units with 17 different floor plans in apartment blocks and detached houses, together with commercial space, offices, recreation facilities, an assisted-living facility for seniors, and child day care centers.

The buildings were partially prefabricated and assembled on-site simply and economically, which minimized construction waste. Any future changes to the flexible structures will likewise generate virtually no waste.

The orientation of the buildings has led to a 30–40 percent reduction in energy consumption compared to complexes of a similar size. Air-conditioning is unnecessary in summer; in winter, heating consists of only two storage heaters per dwelling, which are used only on the coldest days.

The buildings use solar thermal panels to provide hot water, and feature roof gardens, which provide thermal inertia and insulation, especially in the summer. The design of the greenhouses—frames with hatches to allow ventilation and natural thermal conditioning to the building—also plays an important role in saving energy. In addition, rainwater is collected and used for watering plants and filling toilets.

The materials used for both interiors and exteriors are 100 percent environmentally safe. No solvents, additives, or other harmful materials, such as PVC, polyurethane, fiberglass, or resins, were used. Recycled and reused materials are featured throughout.

Each home has an automation system equipped with a touch screen where residents can regulate their energy-reducing mechanisms and security systems.

Photos © Mayte Piera

The entrance to each of the apartment
buildings traces a triangular form on the facade.

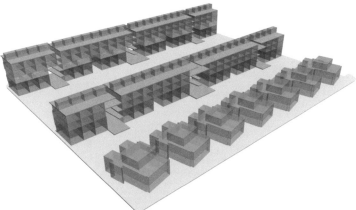

Residential complex rendering

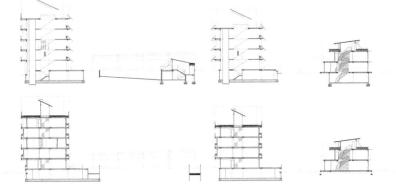

Residential complex section

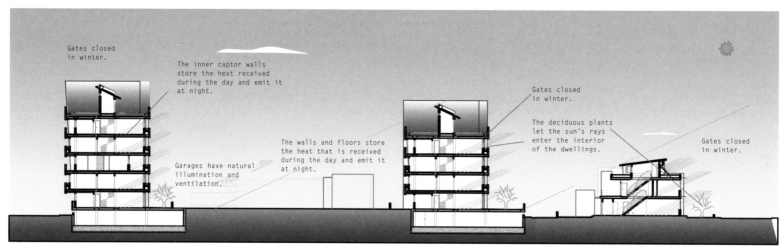

Gates closed
in winter.

The inner captor walls
store the heat received
during the day and emit it
at night.

The walls and floors store
the heat that is received
during the day and emit it
at night.

Garages have natural
illumination and
ventilation.

Gates closed
in winter.

The deciduous plants
let the sun's rays
enter the interior
of the dwellings.

Gates closed
in winter.

Bioclimatic section (winter)

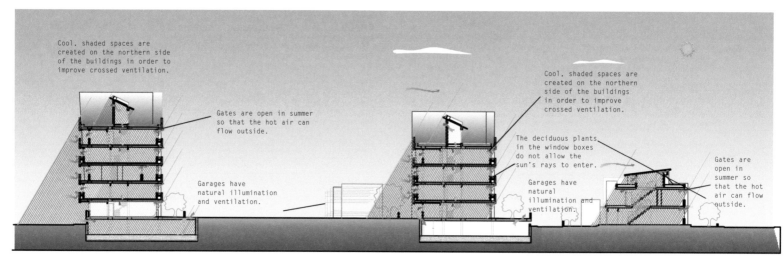

Cool, shaded spaces are
created on the northern side
of the buildings in order to
improve crossed ventilation.

Gates are open in summer
so that the hot air can
flow outside.

Garages have
natural illumination
and ventilation.

Cool, shaded spaces are
created on the northern
side of the buildings
in order to improve
crossed ventilation.

The deciduous plants
in the window boxes
do not allow the
sun's rays to enter.

Garages have
natural
illumination and
ventilation.

Gates are
open in
summer so
that the hot
air can flow
outside.

Bioclimatic section (summer)

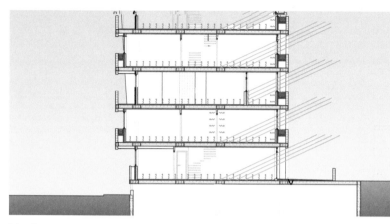

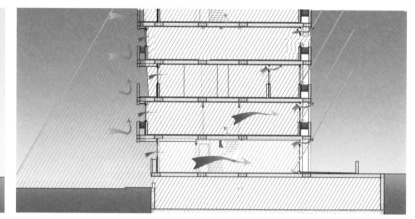

Bioclimatic section (blocks in winter)   Bioclimatic section (blocks in summer)

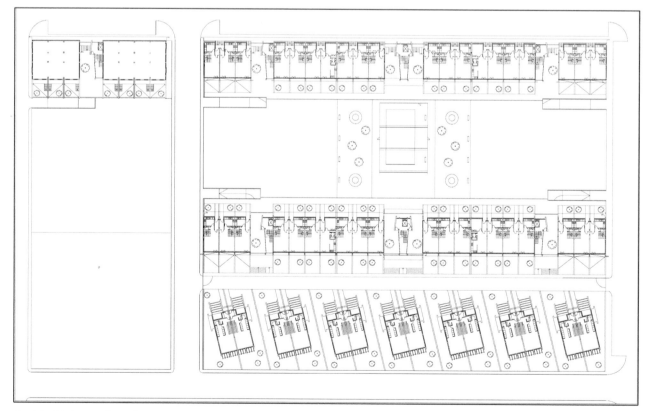

Residential complex plan

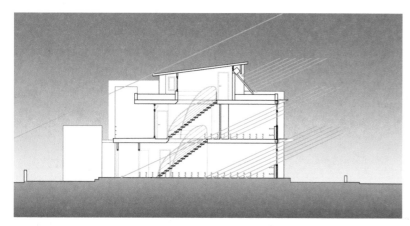

Bioclimatic section (detached houses in winter)

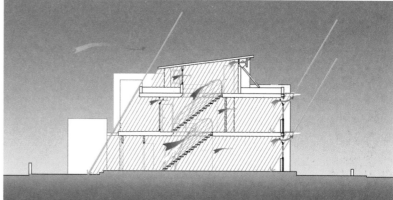

Bioclimatic section (detached houses in summer)

Detached house elevation

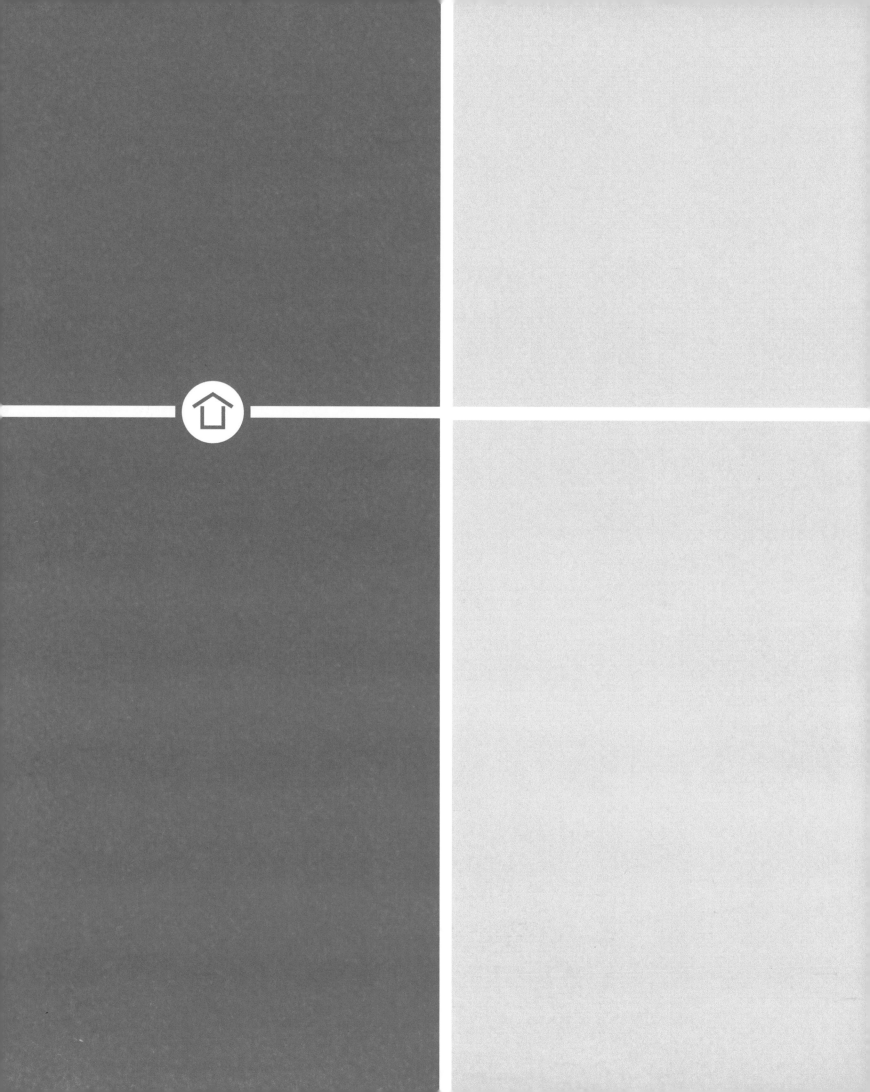

ON-SITE: GREENER HOMES

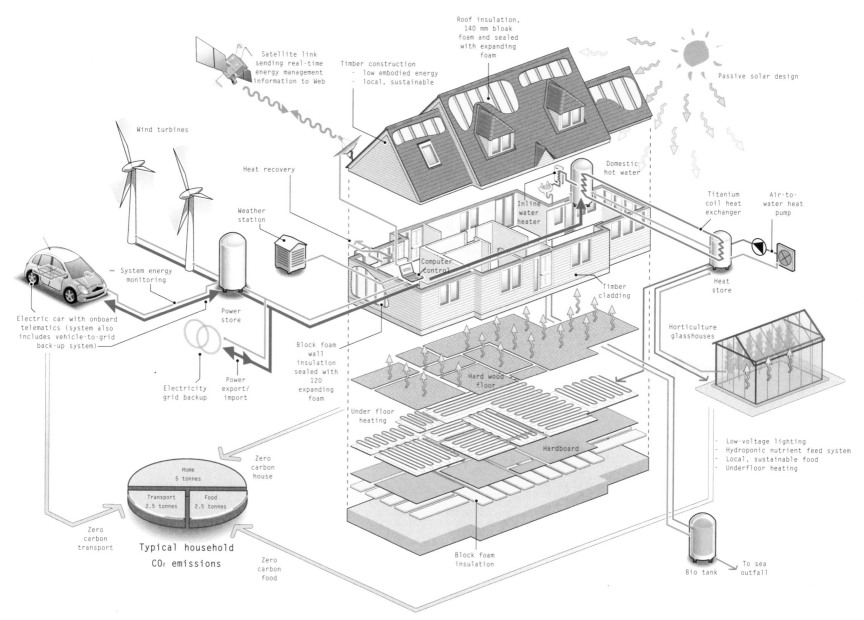

Satellite link sending real-time energy management information to Web

Roof insulation, 140 mm bloak foam and sealed with expanding foam

Timber construction
- low embodied energy
- local, sustainable

Passive solar design

Wind turbines

Heat recovery

Domestic hot water

Titanium coil heat exchanger

Air-to-water heat pump

Weather station

Inline water heater

Electric car with onboard telematics (system also includes vehicle-to-grid back-up system)

System energy monitoring

Computer control

Timber cladding

Heat store

Power store

Electricity grid backup

Power export/ import

Block foam wall insulation sealed with 120 expanding foam

Hard wood floor

Horticulture glasshouses

Under floor heating

Hardboard

- Low-voltage lighting
- Hydroponic nutrient feed system
- Local, sustainable food
- Underfloor heating

Zero carbon house

Home
5 tonnes

Transport
2.5 tonnes

Food
2.5 tonnes

Zero carbon transport

Typical household
CO₂ emissions

Zero carbon food

Block foam insulation

Bio tank

To sea outfall

Bioclimatic illustration

Illustration: www.paulweston.info

ZERO CARBON HOUSE

Ken Fowler, Michael Rea   Shetland, Scotland, UK

 Wind power

Natural materials

Prefabricated construction - Domotics -
Respect for traditional local building styles

Zero Carbon House, a demonstration project of a socio-economic-environmental nature, attempts to show how renewable energy can make a dwelling on the Scottish island of Unst fully self-sufficient. It was designed as an alternative to the CO2 produced by automobile use, fossil fuel combustion, and growing and transporting food.

Located in the Shetland archipelago, this project was cofinanced by private and public institutions such as Communities Scotland, EST Scotland and Shetland Enterprise. Owing to its remote location, materials were shipped from mainland Scotland and England.

The design meets the building code of Unst, characterized by traditional Croft Houses (World Heritage status pending). A prefabricated wooden structure was the base; a number of alterations turned it into a zero-carbon-consuming house.

Because the designers did not opt for a geothermal energy source (mainly for reasons of cost and space), an in-floor radiant heating system was chosen. It is fed by an air-to-water heat pump that extracts heat from the air and transfers it to the water feeding the heating system.

The air in the dwelling is renewed every ninety minutes to ensure that it is filtered and conditioned, improving its quality and preventing problems caused by pollen.

As a complement, a greenhouse is planned next to the dwelling to show that it is possible to grow fruits and vegetables in a self-sufficient way by means of hydroponics.

Lighting the entire house will consume a maximum of 100 watts, thanks to the use of LEDs. Two wind turbines, which have not yet been installed, will supply energy to the house and charge the electric vehicle.

Photos © Philip Andrews

R4 HOUSE

Luis de Garrido   Construmat 2007, Barcelona, Spain

Solar photovoltaic - Passive solar - Solar thermal - Geothermal - Green roof

Natural materials - Reused materials - Recycled materials

Prefabricated construction - Easy disassembly - Domotics - Construction waste minimized

This project, brought to life in Montcada i Reixach outside Barcelona, is an attempt by the architect to create sustainable, attractive, and inexpensive architecture.

Faithful to his motto, "Beauty from the imperfect", the architect sees his objective as the creation of harmonious and appealing objects, while making use of diverse resources and producing minimal waste.

R4 House, presented at Spain's Construmat 2007 construction-industry fair, includes two dwellings built with six shipping containers. There is zero consumption of conventional, fossil fuel-based energy, and practically no waste materials result from the building or disassembly because all the components of both dwellings were designed as modules that are dry-assembled. In this way, if the structure is rebuilt in another location, all of its pieces can be reused.

Many materials were reused, salvaged, or recycled (such as waste from Silestone manufacture that features in floor mosaics, or cullet from the glass-recycling industry used as outdoor paving). The architect-designed system of modules, outfitted in the factory, makes maximum use of materials and panels. At the same time, the modules adapt perfectly to a desired architectural plan.

One of the structures is 1,615 square feet and would cost $82,700 to build; the other, at 323 square feet, could be built for about $16,500. Using shipping containers as the frame ensures flexibility, reuse, and relocation at a very low cost.

As for energy, there are self-regulating systems: a bioclimatic design and optimal use of geothermal collectors and solar energy, with a 1-kilowatt photovoltaic panel in each unit. Construction consumes the least possible energy.

Photos © David Campos, Habitat Futura

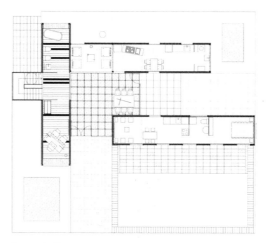

Ground floor

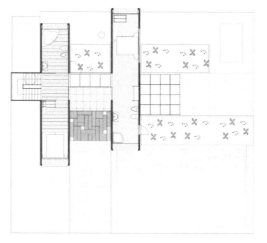

First floor

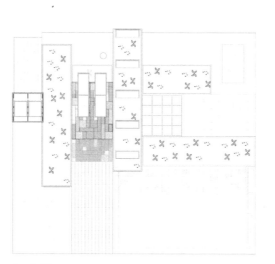

Roof floor

The model exhibited at Construmat 2007 has been permanently installed in Montcada i Reixach, a town close to Barcelona.

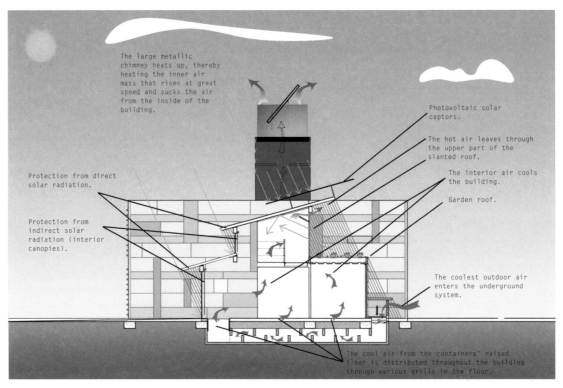

The large metallic chimney heats up, thereby heating the inner air mass that rises at great speed and sucks the air from the inside of the building.

Photovoltaic solar captors.

The hot air leaves through the upper part of the slanted roof.

Protection from direct solar radiation.

The interior air cools the building.

Protection from indirect solar radiation (interior canopies).

Garden roof.

The coolest outdoor air enters the underground system.

The cool air from the containers' raised floor is distributed throughout the building through various grills in the floor.

Bioclimatic section 1 (summer)

Garden roof.

Detail of the screen-printed double glazing.

Thermal solar captors.

Double-glazing with bioclimatic screen-printing prevents the entrance of tangential solar rays.

Facade ventilated with 5cm of insulation.

Cool air penetrates the galleries through holes in the floor.

Bioclimatic section 2 (summer)

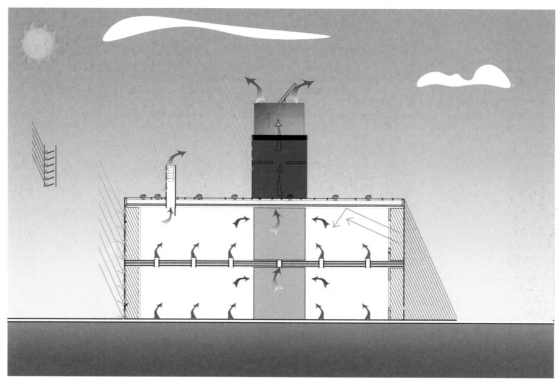

Bioclimatic section 3 (summer)

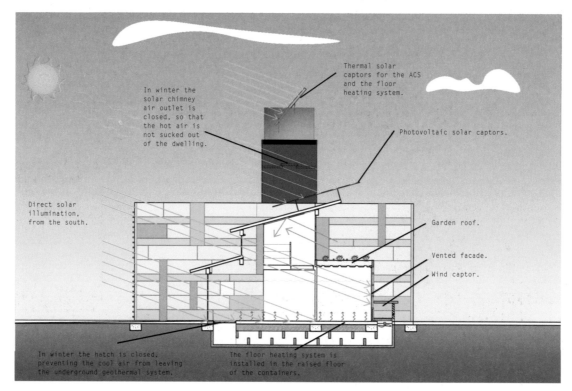

Thermal solar
captors for the ACS
and the floor
heating system.

In winter the
solar chimney
air outlet is
closed, so that
the hot air is
not sucked out
of the dwelling.

Photovoltaic solar captors.

Direct solar
illumination,
from the south.

Garden roof.

Vented facade.

Wind captor.

In winter the hatch is closed,
preventing the cool air from leaving
the underground geothermal system.

The floor heating system is
installed in the raised floor
of the containers.

Bioclimatic section 1 (winter)

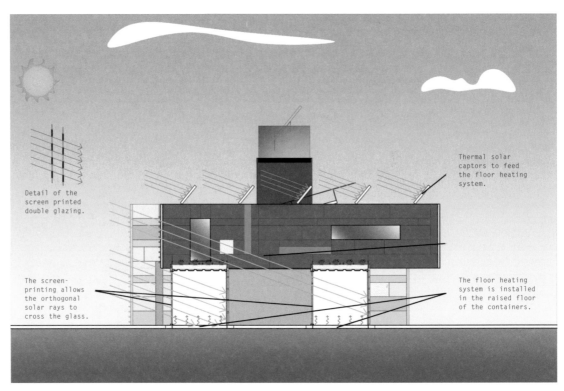

Detail of the
screen printed
double glazing.

Thermal solar
captors to feed
the floor heating
system.

The screen-
printing allows
the orthogonal
solar rays to
cross the glass.

The floor heating
system is installed
in the raised floor
of the containers.

Bioclimatic section 2 (winter)

Bioclimatic section 3 (winter)

DIRECTORY

1+2 Architecture
31 Melville Street, Hobart, Tasmania, 7000 Australia
Tel.: 61 3 6234 8122
Fax: 61 3 6234 8211
mail@1plus2architecture.com
www.1plus2architecture.com

Arkin Tilt Architects
1101 8th Street, Suite 180, Berkeley, CA 94710, USA
Tel.: 1 510 528 9830
Fax: 1 510 528 0206
info@arkintilt.com
www.arkintilt.com

Atelier für Solararchitektur Jordan
Langenharterstrasse 13, 4300 St. Valentin, Austria
Tel.: 43 7435 58706
office@jordan-solar.at
www.jordan-solar.at

att architekten
Markus Gentner
Bauerngasse 12, 90443 Nuremberg, Germany
Tel.: 49 9 1127 44 79 0
Fax: 49 9 1127 44 79 44
mg@att-architekten.de
www.markus-gentner-architekt.de

Baumraum
Andreas Wenning
Roonstrasse 49, 28203 Bremen, Germany
Tel.: 49 421 705 122
a.wenning@baumraum.de
www.baumraum.de

Breathe Architects
Martin Liefhebber + Associates
177 1st Avenue, Toronto, Ontario, M4M 1X3 Canada
Tel.: 1 416 469 0018
Fax: 1 416 469 0987
info@breathebyassociation.com
www.breathebyassociation.com

Cannatà & Fernandes Arquitectos
Rua Freire de Andrade 85, 4250-225 Porto, Portugal
Tel.: 351 228 329 172
Fax: 351 228 329 173
canatafernandes@netcabo.pt
www.cannatafernandes.com

Energy for Sustainable Development (Ltd) ESD
Duncan Price
Fourth Floor, West Entrance
1-3 Dufferin Street, London, EC1Y 8NA, UK
Tel.: 44 20 7628 7722
Fax: 44 20 7382 0369
enquiry@esd.co.uk
www.esd.co.uk
www.zerocarbonhouse.com

EHDD Architecture
500 Treat Avenue Ste. 201, San Francisco, CA 94110, USA
Tel.: 1 415 285 9193
Fax: 1 415 285 3866
sanfrancisco@ehdd.com
www.ehdd.com

Fujy
c/Mallorca 236, Entlo. 1ª, 08008 Barcelona, Spain
Tel.: 34 902 30 33 31
Fax: 34 902 94 70 98
info@fujy.info
www.fujy.info

Jennifer Siegal
1725 Abbot Kinney Blvd., Venice, CA 90291, USA
Tel.: 1 310 439 1129
Fax: 1 310 745 0439
info@designmobile.com
www.designmobile.com

John Friedman Alice Kimm Architects
701 East 3rd Street, Suite 300, Los Angeles, CA 90013, USA
Tel.: 1 213 253 4740
Fax: 1 213 253 4760
info@jfak.net
www.jfak.net

Kieran Timberlake Associates
420 N 20 Street, Philadelphia, PA 19130.3828, USA
Tel.: 1 215 922 6600
Fax: 1 215 922 4680
timberlake@kierantimberlake.com
www.kierantimberlake.com

Leger Wanaselja Architecture
2808 Adeline Street 4, Berkeley, CA 94703, USA
Tel.: 1 510 848 8901
Fax: 1 510 848 8908
lwarc@pacbell.net
www.lwarc.com

LivingHomes
2914 Highland Avenue
Santa Monica, CA 90405
Tel.: 1 310 581 8500
Fax: 1 310 428 9338
info@livinghomes.net
www.livinghomes.net

Luis de Garrido
c/Blasco Ibañez 114, ptas. 7 y 9, 46022 Valencia, Spain
Tel.: 34 96 356 70 70
Fax: 34 96 356 81 81
garrido@mail.ono.es
www.luisdegarrido.com

Michelle Kaufmann Designs
580 2nd Street, Ste 245, Oakland, CA 94607, USA
Tel.: 1 510 271 8015
Fax: 1 510 271 8050
media@mkd-arc.com
www.michellekaufmann.com

Obie G. Bowman
P.O. Box 1114
Healdsburg, CA 95448, USA
Tel./fax: 1 707 433 7833
ogb@sonic.net
www.obiebowman.com

Patrick Marsilli
155 Voie Romaine, 29000 Quimper, France
Tel.: 33 0298 57 60 60
Fax: 33 0298 59 47 29
contact@domespace.com
www.domespace.com

Paul Morgan Architects
Level 10 221 Queen Street, Melbourne, Victoria, 3000 Australia
Tel.: 61 3 9600 3253
Fax: 61 3 9602 5673
office@paulmorganarchitects.com
www.paulmorganarchitects.com

Pelli Clarke Pelli Architects
322 8th Avenue, New York, NY 10001, USA
Tel.: 1 212 417 9496
Fax: 1 212 417 9497
info@pcparch.com
www.pcparch.com

Peter Cardew Architects
1661 Duranleau Street, Vancouver BC, V6H 3S3 Canada
Tel.: 1 604 681 6044
Fax: 1 604 684 6044
general@cardew.ca
www.cardew.ca

Ray Kappe. FAIA
715 Brooktree Road
Pacific Palisades, CA 90272